FAUNA

HAZEL

Robert H. Bendley

New York City 1957

SUZY

THE FLOPHOUSE GANG

AGNES AND FRIEND

Music by

Book and Lyrics by

Published by The Viking Press

dream

RICHARD RODGERS

OSCAR HAMMERSTEIN II

Based on Sweet Thursday *by* JOHN STEINBECK

New York, 1956

Library of Congress catalog card number: 56-7597
Manufactured in U.S.A. by H. Wolff Book Manufacturing Company

DESIGN: Marshall Lee

the cast

in order of their appearance

DOC : William Johnson
HAZEL : Mike Kellin
MILLICENT HENDERSON : Jayne Heller
MAC : G. D. Wallace
SUZY : Judy Tyler
FAUNA : Helen Traubel
JIM BLAIKEY : Rufus Smith
JOHNNY CARRIAGRA : Scotty Engel
PEDRO : Rudolfo Cornejo
RAY BUSCH : John Call
GEORGE HERMAN : Guy Raymond
BILL : Steve Roland
RED : Keith Kaldenberg
WHITEY : Hobe Streiford
DIZZY : Nicolas Orloff
EDDIE : Warren Kemmerling
ALEC : Warren Brown
SONYA : Annabelle Gold
KITTY : Jenny Workman
JOE (THE MEXICAN) : Kenneth Harvey
PANCHO (A WETBACK) : Ruby Braff
AGNES : Temple Texas
MABEL : Jackie McElroy

EMMA : Marilyn Bradley
BEULAH : Mildred Slavin
MARJORIE : Louise Troy
CHO CHO SEN : Pat Creighton
SUMI : Sandra Devlin
SONNY BOY : Joseph Leon
ESTEBAN (A GUITAR-PLAYER) : Jerry LaZarre
A WAITER : Kazimir Kokich
HARRIET : Patricia Wilson
HILDA : Ruth Kobart
FRED : Marvin Krauter
SLICK : Gene Kevin
SLIM : Don Weissmuller
BASHA : Sigyn
BUBBLES : Marsha Reynolds
WEIRDE : Patti Karkalits
DR. DORMODY : Calvin Thomas

and various other incidental characters one might see any day or night on Cannery Row

The names of actors listed above, and the portraits of characters on the end papers, represent the players in the original production. The photographs are by George Karger—Pix.

PIPE DREAM *was first presented by Rodgers and Hammerstein at the Sam S. Shubert Theatre, New York, on November 30, 1955.*

STAGE DIRECTION by Harold Clurman
SCENERY and LIGHTING by Jo Mielziner
COSTUMES by Alvin Colt
ORCHESTRATION by Robert Russell Bennett
MUSICAL DIRECTION by Salvatore dell'Isola
STAGING of dances and musical numbers by Boris Runanin

scenes

time: the present

THE WESTERN BIOLOGICAL LABORATORY

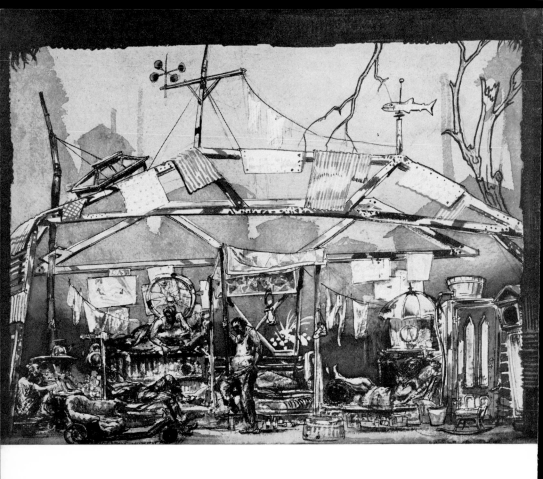

THE PALACE FLOPHOUSE

THE BEAR FLAG CAFE

SONNY BOY'S PIER RESTAURANT

musical numbers

For Elaine and the two Dorothys,
for their tireless supervision

ACT ONE

act one: scene 1

The Western Biological Laboratory.

On the bookshelves are beat-up zoological books; museum jars containing mounted specimens; labeled cardboard boxes and hundreds of small wooden slide boxes; dictionaries, encyclopedias, poetry, and plays. On whatever wall spaces that are not covered with shelves are reproductions of Daumier, Titian, and Leonardo; Picasso, Dali, and George Grosz.

Down right is the door to the street. The outer side of the door faces the audience so that those who visit Doc can be seen before they enter.

Above the door up left is an entrance to another room. Below this an army cot is placed against the left wall of the set. Through the window the light is the blue-gray that presages dawn. As the scene progresses the light increases gradually.

After the overture, the orchestra plays a prelude which continues through the rise of the curtain and blends into the first song.

Doc is at work at a table, center. The only lighting on the stage is concentrated there. On the table are two flat mass jars. One is labeled MALE *and the other* FEMALE. *There is also a row of fairly large watch glasses, and they are numbered from 1 to 10 in red. The microscope is in the center of the table and Doc sits behind it. He takes an occasional swallow from a beer can, beside which stands another, unopened. Doc's tools are eye-droppers and mass rods. He takes a few drops from the jar marked* FEMALE *and squeezes them into a watch glass, adds a few drops from the jar marked* MALE, *consults his watch, which lies on the table before him, makes notes on a working sheet of number and time, stirs mixture gently with the rod, and slides the watch glass under the microscope, studies it for a few seconds, then moves it back into line, consults his sheets, looks at his watch, and shakes a few menthol crystals into another glass.*

Doc is whistling as he works. Meanwhile Hazel has entered downstage. He is a husky, rugged young man. He knocks on the door. Doc looks up but has no time to respond because the door is opened immediately by Hazel.

DOC: Hiya, Hazel baby.

HAZEL: I see your light was on. I thought maybe it was time.

DOC (*looking at his watch*): You're early. Four forty-two. Got ten minutes yet.

HAZEL: I couldn't sleep anyway, We got a new guy at the

Flophouse, George Herman, and he woke me up. He had a nightmare—dreamt he was back with his wife.

DOC: Is that so bad?

HAZEL: Well, you see that's why he moved in with us. She used to wait until he got to sleep and then she'd take a sock at him. Then he'd wake up and knock the hell out of her, and then as soon as he got back to sleep she'd sock him again. That's nerve-wracking!

DOC: I can understand that.

(*Hazel eyes the beer can suggestively. Doc gestures that he may have it. Hazel opens it as he glances out the large window.*)

HAZEL: Why are we goin' to the tide pool? Starfish?

DOC: Got an order for three hundred. Northwestern University.

HAZEL: They got no starfish there?

DOC: They got no ocean there.

HAZEL: Damn if I can see what they want with starfish at a univoisity.

DOC: Idea is, if we study the problem of the starfish, we might find a solution to some of our own.

HAZEL: I don't get the connection.

DOC: Everything is connected. I'll bet the crumbling of a pebble has an effect on everything else in the world—if you could only measure delicately enough.

(*Hazel's brows knit in a painful effort to understand.*)

DOC (*singing*):
    The starfish may look unimportant,
    Lying limply on his underwater shelf.
    He may look unimportant to you,
    But he's very interesting to himself.

    It takes all kinds of people to make up a world,
    All kinds of people and things.
    They crawl on the earth,
    They swim in the sea,
    And they fly through the sky on wings.
    All kinds of people and things,
    And brother, I'll tell you my hunch:
    Whether you like them
    Or whether you don't,
    You're stuck with the whole damn bunch!

    I don't think so much of the buzzard,
    He is something I would never like to be.
    But who knows what goes on in his mind?
    He may think he is superior to me!

HAZEL (*outraged*): Aw now, Doc!

DOC:

You may not admire armadillos,
They're repulsive and they lead peculiar lives.
They may not look attractive to you
But they're very interesting to their wives.

It takes all kinds of people to make up a world,
All kinds of people and things.
They crawl on the earth,
They swim in the sea
And they fly through the sky on wings.
All kinds of people and things,
And brother, I'll tell you my hunch:
Whether you like them
Or whether you don't,
You're stuck with the whole damn bunch!

(*The orchestra resumes playing underneath dialogue. Doc returns to his work. Millicent enters from the next room, wearing a raincoat of Doc's over, presumably, nothing else.*)

MILLICENT: What are you doing out here?

DOC: I've got to go to the tide pool this morning. I told you that before you came over last night. Don't you remember?

MILLICENT: Boy, do you make a girl feel attractive! (*She looks at the two jars.*) Male and female! Male and female what?

DOC: Starfish. Ova; sperm. I've been mixing it in these glasses. At the end of the first half-hour I put menthol crystals in glass number one—to kill the developing embryos. Next half-hour—glass number two. That way I'm getting a series of the developing animal—

MILLICENT: You got up every half-hour? (*She looks back toward the other room.*) How *many* half-hours?

DOC: Four. I set the alarm clock.

MILLICENT: Why didn't it wake *me* up?

DOC (*smiling*): You had quite a little to drink at dinner.

MILLICENT (*looking down at the table*): Looks like the starfish have been having a better time than I have.
(*Hazel laughs. Millicent turns and sees him for the first time.*)

DOC: This is Millicent Henderson. Millicent, I'd like you to meet Hazel.

MILLICENT: Hazel! Maybe that explains the whole thing!
(*She stalks off angrily through the door at left.*)

HAZEL (*following her*): Hey, what do you mean by that? (*He stands in the door and calls through to her*) My mother had eight children in seven years and she got kinda mixed up and she named me Hazel by mistake. Get it?

MILLICENT (*offstage*): No!

HAZEL: Hey Doc! You know what she thinks I am?

DOC: I've got an idea.

HAZEL: She's getting dressed there, right in front of me! She must think—

DOC: What do you care what she thinks?

HAZEL: That's right, what do I care?

(*He leans comfortably against the door and takes a good look offstage. Mac enters from downstage, opens the door and enters Doc's house breathlessly. A girl follows him in.*)

MAC: Doc! I'm glad you're still here!

HAZEL: Whatsamatter, Mac?

MAC: A dame hurt herself—

DOC: Damn it, Mac! I've told all of you—again and again—I'm *not* a *real* doctor! It's illegal to—

(*But Mac has brought Suzy forward. She is a kind of pretty girl without being a classic beauty—a good figure, about twenty-one, medium height. She carries a brown imitation-leather purse in one hand. The other hand has a crude bandage on it. Suzy looks around, sizing up the place and sizing up Doc. Finally she speaks.*)

SUZY: I cut my hand.

DOC (*pity overcoming his sense of legality, as it always does*): Let me see it.

(*She comes forward. He speaks as he takes the bandage off.*)

How did you do this?

SUZY: I broke a store window—(*holding up her metal-clasped handbag*) with this. Some of the glass come off on my hand.

HAZEL (*to Mac*): What store?

MAC: The Chinaman's.

DOC: Why did you do a thing like that?

SUZY: There was food in the window—I took a couple of doughnuts.

(*Doc looks at her*)

I was hungry.

DOC: I see. (*The bandage is off now and he examines the hand.*) Just missed a vein. You're lucky.

SUZY: Am I?

(*Doc goes to the bookcase for his first-aid equipment, gauze, iodine, and so forth. Suzy addresses Mac.*)

Feller at the store didn't *look* like a Chinaman.

MAC: He ain't. He's a Mexican. He bought the store off the Chinaman.

SUZY: Nice feller. He didn't call the cops.

MAC: Maybe he will later.

SUZY: Nope. If a guy don't call the cops right away he don't ever call them.

DOC: What's your name?

SUZY: Suzy.

DOC: This is going to hurt a little.

(*He applies the iodine. Suzy stiffens but doesn't yell.*)

Atta girl, Suzy.

(*She bites her lip and then walks around shaking her hand a little to relieve the pain. She looks into the snake cage.*)

SUZY: Hey! What have you got down there? They look like snakes.

DOC: They are snakes.

(*He beckons to her to come back to him, which she does as she speaks.*)

SUZY: Hey, what kind of a place is this anyway?

MAC (*proudly*): This is the Western Biological Laboratory.

HAZEL: Belongs to Doc there.

SUZY: Yeh?

(*Doc starts to bandage her hand.*)

DOC: After I get this bandage on, you better lie down a while.
Stay as long as you like. I've got to go down to the tide
pool.

SUZY: What's a tide pool?

MAC: It's—you know—a pool. Made out of a circle of rocks.
It's on the furthermost tip of peninsula.

HAZEL: The ocean keeps comin' in and out of it. It's where
Doc catches things!

(*The following lines are sung.*)

MAC:

It's nothin' at all when the tide is high,
It's just a bunch o' waves.

HAZEL:

They whip all around all 'a rocks
An' chase all 'a fish into caves.

DOC:

But if you get there when the tide is low

And the pool is clear and clean,
You can see to the bottom—

HAZEL:

The damn'dest collection o' creeps you ever seen!

DOC:

Hungry flowers that live on fish,
Scooping in whatever comes,
Crabs that grab another crab
And chew his legs.

SUZY:

The dirty bums!

HAZEL:

Starfish, havin' himself a lunch,
Eats a mussel off a shell.

MAC:

Shrimps 'n limpets 'n snails 'n eels,
What a smelly tale they tell—
Fightin' each other
'N eatin' each other
'N lousin' up the sea!

HAZEL:

Stupid sons o' fishes,
If you're askin' me!

DOC:

Out on the top of the water
Everything seems all right.
There's a sun on the bay at daytime
And a moon on the bay at night.

MAC:

A breeze blows in from offa the reef
An' you hear the whistlin' buoy—

HAZEL:

While Doc an' me are chewin' the fat
An' talkin' a lot o' hooey.

DOC, MAC, AND HAZEL:

Out on the top of the water
It's quieter than a well;
While under the water, under the water,
They're raising holy hell!

(*Hazel and Mac get together, wave their four arms, and
"make like an octopus."*)

DOC:

Get a load of the octopus!
Looking for a crab to eat,
Oozes out of slimy weeds,
Creeping on his floppy feet.

MAC:

Crab too busy to see him come,
Crab's a cinch to catch because
He is chewin' another crab,
Strugglin' in his greedy claws—

DOC, MAC, AND HAZEL:

Fighting each other
And eating each other
And lousing up the sea,

Fighting and feeding
And mating and breeding
And filling up the sea,
Stupid sons o' fishes!
Stupid sons o' fishes!
Stupid sons o' fishes!
   To live in a *TIDE POOL!*

SUZY: Octopusses, huh? What do you do with all those things?

DOC: I sell 'em. (*Leading Suzy over to the cot*) Now you rest there a while.

SUZY: Guess you make pretty good dough, huh, Doc? (*Looking out the window from the cot*) That your convertible out there?

DOC: No, that's—

(*The answer enters in the person of Millicent, now dressed to go, and very fashionably too. After a scornful look at Suzy and the others she addresses Doc.*)

MILLICENT: Thank you for a perfectly lovely time! It's been a peachy date from start to finish—(*looking at Suzy*) and I just love your friends.

SUZY: I ain't a friend. I'm a patient of the doctor's.

DOC (*to Millicent*): She came in to get her hand fixed up.

MILLICENT: Really?

(*She starts for the door.*)

SUZY: And what did *you* come in to get fixed up, sister?

(*This one is hard for Millicent to answer, so she dashes out, slamming the door.*)

DOC (*to Suzy quietly*): Why the hell did you talk to her like that?

SUZY: I don't know why the hell I talked to her like that. Guess maybe I figured you had more class than to be mixed up with a bum.

DOC: She's not a bum.

SUZY: That yellow convertible don't fool me. I can tell a bum a mile off. Okay, it's none of my business.

DOC: Okay.

(*He goes upstage and starts putting on his rubber boots. Mac returns to his chair, his beer, and his silent thoughts.*)

SUZY: Why should I worry about you, anyway? A guy who lives with snakes and bugs and things. Must be something wrong with a guy like that.

DOC: Something wrong with most people. Might even be something wrong with you, tootsie.

SUZY: There's plenty wrong with me . . . but I don't spend my life scroungin' around in the mud for a lot of lousy starfish. What's the matter? Haven't you got the guts to live like you ought to live?

HAZEL: Can I give her a crack in the mouth, Doc?

(*Doc shakes his head and walks over to Suzy, putting on his coat.*)

DOC: I'm living just the way I want to live. Is that okay with you?

SUZY: No, by God. It ain't okay with me!

DOC: Well, that's just too damn bad!

SUZY: Fix your sleeves!

(*She points to the sleeves of his coat, which were rolled up by Millicent when she borrowed it.*)

DOC (*angrily pulling down his sleeves*): Let's get straight about one thing. The work I'm doing—(*He has looked at his watch.*) Damn it, look at the time! Tide's been out eight minutes already! This is what I get for arguing with a silly dame who puts her hand through glass windows.
(*Doc and Hazel start picking up buckets and other paraphernalia they are taking with them.*)

SUZY: I wish you luck. I hope you catch an octopus with a million legs and sell it for a dollar a leg!

DOC (*coming down to her, carrying his buckets*): Look! (*He measures his words carefully, trying to control his temper.*) There is no big money in what I am doing.

SUZY: Then what are you doing it for?

DOC: I'm trying to find out things that might be important to the science of invertebratology.
(*Pause.*)

SUZY: All right. Then what?

DOC (*stuck for a moment*): What do you mean, then what?

SUZY: I mean then what! What'll you do?
(*Pause. He fights his way out of a corner.*)

DOC: I'll write a paper, that's what I'll do!

MAC (*coming back to life at this momentous news*): That right, Doc?

SUZY: What'll you do with it after you write it?

DOC: I'll . . . probably read it before some scientific society.

HAZEL: Holy mackerel!

SUZY: What'll it be about—octopusses?

DOC: It might very likely be about octopusses.
  (*He assumes as much dignity as he can, and starts for the door.*)

MAC: You never done nothin' like that before.

HAZEL: What are you goin' to call it, Doc?

DOC: What the hell's the difference what I call it?

HAZEL (*following him*): Only asking—
  (*When Doc gets to the door Suzy calls to him.*)

SUZY: Hey, Doc!
  (*He looks back over his shoulder.*)
  Thanks for fixing my hand.
  (*Without answering her, Doc turns and goes out with Hazel and slams the door.*)

MAC: What you need, sister, is a good kick in the pants.

SUZY (*rising from the cot*): No I don't. (*She crosses toward the window.*) I had plenty kicks in the pants. (*She looks out the window.*) Why do you call him Doc? He ain't a real doctor, I heard him say.

MAC: No, but he knows plenty. We hustle him all the time, but baby we don't let no outsiders take him. He's ours.

SUZY: What's he got that anybody wants?

MAC: He fixed your hand, didn't he? Last week one of the dames at the Bear Flag gets the hiccups for two days. She comes to Doc.

SUZY (*looking out window*): Bear Flag Cafe. That the place across the street—where the lights are still on?

MAC: Yeh.

SUZY: He go there much?

MAC: Doc? No, he don't ever go to no place like that. He plays it different.

SUZY: Stuff like that yellow convertible, huh?

MAC: All kinds of dames fall for him.

SUZY: I didn't.

MAC (*studying her*): Oh, you're too smart.

SUZY: I ain't smart. I just ain't that dumb.

(*She walks up and down. Her hand seems to hurt her a little bit.*)

MAC: Whyn't you lay down and recrooperate like the Doc said?

SUZY: Don't feel like layin' down. Kinda jumpy from the trip—ridin' all night.

MAC: Good trip?

SUZY: Lousy.

(*She sings*)

Scooted outa Frisco over Route One-O-One,
Bummed a ride as far as San Jose,
Rode aboard a Greyhound till I run outa dough,
Landed on my can in Monterey!

But I see a lotta things along the way
And I did a lotta thinkin' on the way . . .

I rode by a house
With the windows lighted up,
Lookin' brighter than a Christmas tree,
 And I said to myself
 As I rode by myself,
 Everybody's got a home but me.

I rode by a house
Where the moon was on the porch
And a girl was on her feller's knee,
 And I said to myself
 As I rode by myself,
 Everybody's got a home but me.

I am free
And I'm happy to be free,
To be free in the way I want to be,

But once in a while,
When the road is kinda dark
And the end is kinda hard to see,
 I look up and I cry
 To a cloud goin' by,
 Won't there ever be a home for me, somewhere?
 Everybody's got a home but me.

(She speaks)

You live in a house around here?

M A C *(taking Suzy over to door and pointing)*: You can just see it. Top of the hill, see?

S U Z Y : No. All I can see is somethin' that looks like a little warehouse.

M A C : That's it. Used to be for storin' fish meal when the Chinaman had it. I and eight other fellers live there. We call it the Palace Flophouse.

S U Z Y *(laughing)*: The Palace Flophouse.

M A C : You can still smell the fish meal a little, but we—live there.

S U Z Y : Sure. You hardly ever meet somebody who don't live somewhere.

(She goes to get her bag from the table.)

M A C : Where you goin' to go?

S U Z Y : I don't know.

M A C : I guess you'll land on your feet somehow.

S U Z Y *(defiantly)*: I *am* on my feet.

(She sings)

I am free
And I'm happy to be free,
To be free in the way I want to be.
(Mac nods his head and smiles wryly)
But once in a while,
When I'm talkin' to myself
And there's no one there to disagree,
    I look up and I cry

To the big empty sky,
Won't there ever be a home for me, somewhere?
Everybody's got a home but me!

(*Suzy resumes pacing up and down and Mac watches her thoughtfully. Fauna enters on the street, knocks on the door, and opens it immediately, just like everybody else.*)

MAC: Hiya, Fauna.

FAUNA: Hi, Mac. (*Going over to Suzy*) You the girl got hurt? I heard you was here.

SUZY: It don't take long for news to get around this place!

MAC: What you got there, Fauna?

FAUNA: Some whisky a feller makes up in Pine Canyon. Before I buy it I wanted Doc to test.

MAC (*taking the bottle*): Doc ain't here. Let me test it. If I die don't buy it.

(*He takes a swig. Fauna walks back to Suzy and looks down at her bandaged hand.*)

FAUNA: Must of been pretty hungry.

(*Suzy doesn't answer. Fauna looks uncomfortable. She is soft-hearted and feels guilty if she doesn't help somebody who needs help.*)

I'd like to help you, but business is off at my place. (*pointing through the window*) I run the Bear Flag Cafe across the street.

(*Suzy nods*)

Ah, it'd be against my better judgment, anyway. There's something about you. I don't know what it is, but **you** wouldn't be right. (*Balked by Suzy's disconcerting silence, she turns back to Mac.*) Well, Mac, what do you say? How does it taste?

MAC: It ain't exactly what I'd call a taste. It's more like a burn —or a cut.

(*Jim Blaikey enters. He is a plain-clothes cop.*)

FAUNA: Hello, Jim.

JIM: Hiya, Fauna. (*He exchanges a wave with Mac. Suzy tightens up. A cop! She senses it, and tries to look unconcerned as Jim walks over to her.*)

This the girl that was run down by a store window?

FAUNA: Yep!

(*Suzy holds up her bandaged hand.*)

JIM: Know anybody in town?

SUZY: I got an aunt here.

JIM: What's her name?

SUZY: That your business? You a cop?

(*Jim nods.*)

All right, I don't have an aunt.

JIM: Social Security card?

SUZY: Lost it.

(*Pause.*)

JIM: If you need a buck to blow town, I'll give it to you.

SUZY: I think I'll look around a little.

JIM: Tough place to get a job since the cannery closed.

(*Suzy doesn't answer.*)

My advice is to get out. If I see you hanging around the street it won't be advice any more. In fact, sister—

FAUNA (*breaking in quickly*): Jim! I—I'm taking her in with
　me.
　(*Pause. Jim turns to Suzy.*)
JIM: That right? You going with Fauna?
SUZY: I guess so.
JIM (*to Fauna*): You're slippin', Fauna.
FAUNA: Hell, I can't see what I got 'til I wash her up!
　(*Jim starts for door.*)
　So long, Jim!
MAC: See you, Jim!
　(*The others wave "so long" and Jim goes out. Fauna and
　Suzy face each other.*)
FAUNA: Well, now I'm stuck with you.
SUZY: You don't have to be.
FAUNA: Where else you got to go?
SUZY: No place.
FAUNA: What's your name?
SUZY: Suzy.
FAUNA: Mine's Fauna.
SUZY: That's a funny name.
MAC: The Doc give it to her when she first came here.
FAUNA: I told him my name was Flora and he said I looked
　more like a Fauna.
　(*Suzy laughs. Music of "Everybody's Got a Home" starts
　here and continues beneath dialogue for rest of scene.*)
SUZY: That Doc—he's a funny kind of guy.
　(*Fauna looks at Suzy appraisingly.*)
FAUNA: When the stores open we'll go down and get you

something to wear. Got to go to work on your hair, too. . . .
How long since you had something to eat?

SUZY: Yesterday.

FAUNA: C'mon. We'll go over to the Bear Flag and fry our-
selves some eggs.

SUZY: Thanks. (*She starts to follow Fauna, then turns and
looks back at the room.*) Can you imagine that Doc living
all by himself here, with snakes and starfish and octopusses?

MAC: It's the way he likes it.

(*Fauna studies Suzy.*)

SUZY: Yeh, I guess so. But boy! Somebody ought to clean this
place up for him. Sure needs a cleaning.

FAUNA (*drily*): Yeh. Sure does. Get goin', kid.

(*As the refrain comes up to its end, Fauna and Suzy file out
the door. Mac puts out the lights.*)

act one: scene 2

Cannery Row, a few weeks later.

As the lights go up Jim Blaikey is whistling the refrain of "All Kinds of People."

Two little boys enter—Johnny Carriagra and Pedro. One is carrying a baseball bat, the other a glove and baseball.

JOHNNY: Hiya, Jim.

JIM: Hi, kids.
  (*As the boys exit, Ray Busch, an insignificant-looking man, enters and waves to Jim tentatively.*)
  Anything I can do for you?

RAY: I'm looking for a place called the Palace Flophouse.

JIM (*pointing*): You go past the Bear Flag Cafe—

RAY: I think I heard of that.

JIM: You probably have. But you go past it anyway. Turn left and walk up the hill and you'll bump right into the Palace Flophouse.

RAY: Thanks.
  (*He starts to go.*)

JIM: You lookin' for somebody?

RAY: My brother-in-law. He went there two weeks ago.

JIM: That'd be George Herman.

RAY (*surprised*): That's right.

JIM: Know any of the other fellers there? Whitey? . . . Mac?
(*Ray shakes his head.*)
Know Hazel?

RAY: They got a girl up there?

JIM: Hazel's a man.

RAY: They sound like a funny crowd.
(*He goes off. Mac enters.*)

JIM: Hey, Mac!

MAC: Hiya, Jim.

JIM: What are you lookin' so worried about?

MAC: Give you three guesses.

JIM: About Doc, huh?
(*Mac nods.*)
I never see Cannery Row so upset about anything. According' to what everybody says, all the fun has gone out of Doc. What started him off on this kick?

MAC: Remember the night the dame got her hand cut at the Chinaman's?
(*Jim nods.*)
Well, she and Doc got into an argument and she asks him, what's he doin'. All of a sudden it comes over him that he ain't doin' nothin'—so to cover up he tells her he's goin' to write this damn paper.

JIM: Now he's stuck with it, huh?

MAC: That's the way I figger it. 'Course Doc kids himself that he's likin' what he's doin'—says he's got direction at last—don't go around in circles no more.

JIM: Funny thing to say.

MAC: Why shouldn't a guy go around in circles like everybody else?

JIM: What are you goin' to do about it, Mac?

MAC: I been cogitating on an idea. It ain't good enough to tell anybody yet. Got a lot of bugs in it. Somethin' to do with he just told me he can't write the paper good unless he gets some particular kind of a new big powerful microscope.

JIM: How much does a thing like that cost?

MAC: About three hundred dollars.

JIM: How you goin' to get that?

MAC: That's one of the bugs I told you about.

(*He starts off.*)

JIM: Good luck to you, Mac.

(*Mac waves in acknowledgement and exits, as the refrain of "All Kinds of People" starts. Jim, looking off after Mac, sings*)

One guy will kill you for dough,
And one guy will rob you of lunch,
One guy will help and he makes you fall
In love with the whole darn bunch.

(*He exits as the lights fade.*)

act one: scene 3

The Palace Flophouse, immediately following previous scene.

A room with two windows placed very high on the wall. There is an entrance to the outside left. The walls are whitewashed. The furniture is the result of sporadic collections of pieces having no relation to one another. There is an army cot, a mattress set on rusty springs, and another mattress set on nothing. Another bed is an uncompleted four-poster, the posts being two-by-fours. There is a wicker chaise longue painted bright red; a grandfather clock without dial, face, or works. The pictures on the walls are mostly calendars showing improbable, luscious blondes holding bottles of Coca-Cola, etc. A bundle of gilded cattails stands in one corner, and a sheaf of peacock feathers is nailed to the wall beside the grandfather clock. A hanging kerosene lamp attests to the lack of electricity.

The most striking article is the stove, a silver-scrolled monster with floriated warming ovens and a front like a nickel-plated tulip garden. Vines of morning glories grow up outside the windows, and through the door can be seen several fuchsia bushes planted in five-gallon cans.

Hazel is at work on his four-poster bed, which he is in the process of building. Whitey lies on an army cot polishing his favorite instrument, a bongo drum. Bill sits on the bunk, playing a guitar and humming "The Tide Pool" refrain. On the mattress George Herman sits holding on to his knees, listening to the music and contemplating life in general. His head turns slowly toward Hazel's bed.

GEORGE: Gettin' to look pretty.

HAZEL: I'm buildin' the whole thing from memory . . . saw one like it in a movin' picture 'bout a year ago.
(*Ray appears in the doorway. He doesn't come in very far, but stands there timidly. George turns and sees him.*)

RAY: Hello, George.

GEORGE: What you doin' here, Ray?

RAY: Sally says to come home.

GEORGE: You tell her I ain't comin'. I been sleepin' good here. Nobody beats me up in the middle of the night.

RAY: Personally, I think you'd be screwy if you went back to her. (*He looks around.*) So this is the Palace Flophouse? First time I seen it.
(*Mac enters. He looks disconsolate. All heads turn toward him as if to say: "Any news?" Mac sits on the nearest bed, silent for a few moments.*)

HAZEL: Did you see Doc?
(*Mac nods.*)
What did he have to say?

MAC: Nuthin'. He ain't got time to talk these days. I drunk a can of beer and then I took off. He was workin' all the time.

HAZEL: What was he doin'?

MAC: Well, he's got these two octopusses in a tank on the table in front of him. He sits and studies 'em. Then he writes a few words down on a piece of paper. Then he peruses the octopusses again.

(*Mac rests his chin on his fist, imitating Doc.*)

RAY: What can a man write about octopusses?

MAC: He's got an idea they get nervous breakdowns, like people.

RAY: I don't think a man can make any money writin' about octopusses havin' nervous breakdowns.

(*Mac looks curiously at Ray.*)

GEORGE: Mac, this is my brother-in-law, Ray. He's a business-man.

(*Mac and the others turn their heads toward Ray as if he were something unique and scarcely believable. They make him feel that an explanation is due.*)

RAY: I work for a concern.

GEORGE: He works all the time, fifty-two weeks a year.

(*Mac looks at Ray with shocked incredulity.*)

HAZEL: That sounds awful.

MAC: Sure does.

HAZEL: I mean about Doc. You gotta do somethin', Mac.

MAC: I been givin' it a lot of thought.

HAZEL: What do you figger is goin' to happen to him, Mac?

MAC: I figger he's goin' to keep workin' on that lousy paper and he ain't never goin' to finish it.

HAZEL: Why not?

MAC: It's sumpin' we gotta face, Hazel. Doc don't know how to write a paper!

HAZEL: Mac, I want you should step outside with me and put up your dukes.

MAC: Whatsa matter?

HAZEL: You can't treat Doc that way. Not Doc.

MAC: What way am I treating him? I ain't done nothin' to Doc.

HAZEL: You said he **can't** write that paper. That's what you done.

(The situation is interrupted and relieved by the entrance of Eddie, carrying a large jug, followed by Alec. Whitey takes advantage of the interruption by coming in between Hazel and Mac.)

WHITEY: Look fellers! There's Eddie!

(All heads turn toward Eddie.)

GEORGE: What you got in the jug today, Eddie?

EDDIE: Oh, a little gin and bourbon and red wine.

RAY: Is that a good combination?

EDDIE: Try it.

(He hands the jug to Ray, who barely gets it to his lips before Red takes it away from him.)

RED: Good, huh? *(He takes a good swig himself.)*

GEORGE (*to Ray, while Whitey and Mac take long swallows*):
Eddie works over at the Bear Flag. He keeps that jug under
the bar and pours in whatever the customers leave in their
glasses.

HAZEL (*to Mac*): Wasn't we goin' outside?

MAC (*innocently*): What for?

HAZEL (*stumped*): Somethin' about Doc.

(*He rubs his head to try to figure out what it was. Mac
takes advantage of the memory lapse and grabs the jug
from Whitey. The boys all gather around, knowing that
Mac is about to make a speech.*)

MAC: Fellers, I want to tell you all somethin' about this guy
Hazel. If I was in trouble I wouldn't want him to do no
figurin', but I sure would like to have him for a friend.
(*Hazel bows his head in embarrassment.*)
I make a solemn move we all stand up and drink a silent
toast to Hazel, as noble a guy as you'll ever meet.

BOYS: To Hazel.

HAZEL: Aw, hell, fellers.

(*He wipes a tear from his eyes with his sleeves. The boys
all stand in a circle around him and pass the jug from one
to another.*)

MAC (*drinking*): To Hazel!

GEORGE (*drinking*): To Hazel!

HAZEL: Could somebody make a toast to somebody else, so
I can get a drink?

MAC: Sure thing. (*He takes the jug and makes a solemn toast.*)

To Yogi Berra!
(*Mac drinks, passes Hazel the jug, and turns to Ray.*)

MAC: That right about you working fifty-two weeks a year?

RAY: Sure. Don't you have to work to eat?
(*The boys exchange looks with one another.*)
Don't anybody here work?

MAC: Every now and then one of us takes a job. Eddie here
works at the Bear Flag bar right now.
(*Ray turns to Hazel.*)

RAY: Don't you work?

HAZEL: Me? No. I ain't got the time.
(*The following lines are sung.*)

MAC:
What do you do all day, Ray?
What do you do all day?

RAY:
I wake at six
And take my wife
Her breakfast on a tray.

I walk the kids to school,
Then I run to catch a bus—

MAC:

That's the life for us, boys!

ALL:

That's the life for us!

WHITEY:

Then what, Ray?

GEORGE:

Tell the boys, Ray.

RAY:

I work all day on an adding machine,
Adding the boss's dough.
At six o'clock I am back on a bus,
Back to my home I go.
My supper I sup,
I feel so beat up
I'm soon asleep in my bed.

MAC:

When you grow old and die, Ray,
How will you know you're dead?

ALL:

When you grow old and die, Ray,
How will you know you're dead?

ALEC:

If you work like a horse till the day you're dead,
You're a part of a horse
And it ain't the head!

GEORGE:

This is the kind of a day I like,
When questions of life are philosophied
By thoughtful companions, sittin' around
And gettin' a little bit ossified.

BILL:

Life is a bowlful of cherries—

WHITEY:

Except when the cherries ain't there.

MAC:

Life is a room full o' feathers
That keep gettin' in your hair.

BILL:

You said it, Mac!

ALEC:

You got it, Mac!

RED:

You hit it right on the button!

GEORGE:

We always keep goin', but where do we go?

BILL:

What do we know?

HAZEL:

Nuttin'.

MAC:

On a lopsided, ramshackle bus
We ride from day to day.
We bounce and we bump and we rattle along.

We rattle along on our way.
Every year it's a hassle for us
To get from June to May.
But somehow or other, by hook or by crook,
We rattle along on our way.
    Every time that we start to fall all apart
    And we're near the end of our rope,
    A screwball comes through with a gimmick that's new
    And our hearts go crazy with hope!
We hop on our lopsided bus
And chase another day,
As happy as candles that shine on a cake,
As gay as the bells on a sleigh!
We rattle along,
Rattle along,
Rattle along on our way.

ALL:

On a lopsided, ramshackle bus
We ride from day to day—

(*They are interrupted by Ray who has broken into the group.*)

MAC: Wait a minute, fellers.

RAY: I think there is someone knocking at the door!
(*Mac pushes Ray toward the door.*)

MAC: Well, answer it!
(*The singing continues.*)

ALL:

Every year it's a hassle for us
To get from June to May—

*(The song is again interrupted by the entrance of Kitty
and Sonya, who carry clothes baskets full of laundry.)*

SONYA: Will a couple of you fellers help us with the clothes
line?

*(The music has continued and the two girls are suddenly
whirled into the craziest of dances by the Flophouse boys.
They find themselves being tossed around and whirled high
in the air; the dainty lingerie in the wash baskets is tossed
around and displayed in amusing fashion by the gang. The
girls manage to rescue these articles, get them back in the
baskets, and rush off. The boys make courtly farewell bows
and resume singing.)*

ALL:

On a lopsided, ramshackle bus
We ride from day to day.

MAC:

We wobble around on a rock-happy road
And rattle along on our way.

ALL:

Every year it's a hassle for us
To get from June to May.

But somehow or other, by hook or by crook,
We rattle along on our way.

BILL:

    When the engine won't work 'n it's goin' berserk
    And we're near the end of our rope,
    We fix up the thing with an old piece of string—

HAZEL:

    And our hearts get lousy with hope!

ALL:

    We hop on our lopsided bus
    And chase another day,
    As happy as candles that shine on a cake,
    As gay as the bells on a sleigh!
    We rattle along,
    Rattle along,
    Rattle along on our way.
    We rattle along,
    Rattle along—
    And try to find our way . . .

GEORGE (*handing Mac the jug*): Better have another, Mac. (*After taking a swig, Mac throws the jug to another thirsty man and addresses the gathering impressively.*)

MAC: Gentlemen, we have a problem.

(*There is a stir, and then silence while everyone listens to what is obviously going to be an important pronunciamento.*)

I been waitin' for a time like this, when we was all together

and relaxed and clear-headed. (*Turning to George*) George, would you mind askin' your brother-in-law to leave us for a while? This is private, only for members.
(*George nods to Ray. Ray starts out.*)

ALEC: What's worryin' you, Mac?
(*They all listen intently.*)

MAC: A. A couple months ago the Mexican purchased the store off the Chinaman, right?

HAZEL: Right.

MAC: B. Question: Does the Mexican know that this buildin' we live in belongs to the store property that he purchased? (*Pause. An exchange of worried looks.*)

ALEC: He never come to collect no rent, so maybe he don't know.

MAC: Maybe he don't. But when the tax bills come around maybe he'll find out.

HAZEL (*who has been working up indignation all by himself*): This Mexican can't take our home away from us! That's against the law! . . . Ain't it?

MAC: No, Hazel. I do not think that would be the dictum of a legal judge.

HAZEL: If he sets foot in that door and opens his yap I'll crack his head open with an iron pipe.

MAC: Now, Hazel, that *is* against the law.

HAZEL: Ain't a man's home like his castle?

WHITEY: Yes, but—
(*Fauna appears in the doorway, a sheaf of papers in her hand.*)

FAUNA: Where's Hazel?

HAZEL: Whatsamatter?

FAUNA: I gotta talk to you.

(*She sits on a bed. The boys sense something important in the air.*)

Remember how I wrote down your birthday date and where you was born and everythin'?

HAZEL: My horror scope! Did you figger it out?

FAUNA: Yes. (*She turns to Mac.*) It's somethin' I can't hardly believe, only I never knew the stars to be wrong.

HAZEL: What do the stars say about me?

FAUNA (*measuring her words*): They say you're going to be President of the United States!

(*An ominous silence greets this announcement. People exchange frightened looks.*)

I know it's crazy but there it is. That's what it says.

WHITEY: I wonder where we could all go?

EDDIE: Hazel, if you love your country, drop dead!

MAC: You musta loused up those figgers, Fauna.

FAUNA (*shaking her head*): I checked and rechecked. (*To Hazel*) How many toes you got?

HAZEL: Nine.

FAUNA: Four on the right foot?

HAZEL: Three!

FAUNA: I'll go over the stuff once more.

(*With a dubious sigh, she starts to study her figures. Everyone is anxious to help her come to another conclusion. At this point Ray appears in the doorway.*)

RAY: Hey, two fellers comin' up the hill. One guy's carryin' a trumpet.

ALEC (*looking out*): It's the Mexican!

(*Hazel picks up a weapon.*)

MAC: Take it easy, Hazel. Remember, you got somethin' to live up to now.

ALEC: The kid with the trumpet looks like one of his wet-backs.

MAC: We gotta be cagey with this feller. Don't give away nothin'. I'll try to ask him a couple of questions. (*To Hazel*) And whatever you do, Hazel—

(*He breaks off as Joe, the Mexican, appears in the doorway.*)

JOE: Afternoon, gentlemen.

(*Some nod and some mumble vague responses. All are on their guard. Pancho, a young Mexican with a trumpet, stands behind Joe.*)

JOE: Hiya, Fauna.

FAUNA: Hi, Joe!

JOE: I heard you was here, Fauna, and I want to do you a favor.

FAUNA: Thanks.

JOE: I have here a genius. (*All heads turn toward Pancho.*) I want you to hear what he can do to a trumpet. (*To Eddie*) He could play in The Bear Flag bar. Customers would tip him, no?

EDDIE: You can't tell what they might do late at night.

JOE: 'Course, I would have to be there to collect for him, so he is not cheated.

FAUNA: You sure treat those wetbacks good.

JOE: My countrymen! I get 'em all jobs. Of course, each one is a different problem. You take Pancho. He is a musician. He must practice, but he cannot practice in my cellar. Police or somebody might hear.

EDDIE: So where does he practice?

JOE: Down on the beach. There is a sewer pipe. I make him blow his trumpet into that.

FAUNA: That explains the mystery. Last Friday nobody could figure it out. Every toilet in the neighborhood give off with "Stormy Weather."

(*At a signal from Joe, Pancho gives out with a hot lick.*)

Bring him around tonight. We'll see how the customers like him.

JOE: Good! They will like him! (*To Mac*) Well! Gotta go back to the store. Got a tax expert comin' to meet me.

(*Sudden silence fills the room.*)

MAC (*with elaborate casualness*): Real-estate taxes?

(*All heads turn slowly toward Joe to wait for the answer.*)

JOE: No, income taxes.

(*A wave of relief sweeps over the gang.*)

The government thinks I owe them money.

MAC: Oh, they got a lotta bums in that Revenue Department.

JOE: I got Doc to look over my figures. You know what? He agrees with the government!

FAUNA (*looking up from her work*): Anybody notice anything funny about Doc lately?

MAC: Sure, everybody's noticed.

JOE: I say it must be a girl. Either he's got one he don't want, or he needs one he ain't got.

HAZEL: Doc don't need no girl. He's always got three or four broads hangin' around his place.

EDDIE: Sure, what do you think he is—a celebrate?

FAUNA (*with a faraway look in her eye*): Does anybody know what day Doc was born? He come from Chicago, I think.

JOE: I can tell you the horoscope without looking in no book. If the man is in trouble, it is on account of a woman.
(*Pancho picks up the introduction with a brilliant lick on the trumpet. Joe starts to sing.*)

You may be a wise and intelligent man,
A genius type of joe—
But if a dumb tomato comes after you,
You'll forget whatever you know.
    You can dodge a stick or a stone,
      You can duck a punch when it's thrown,
      But you can't get away from a dumb tomato
    When she wants you for her own.

(*While the men repeat this refrain, Joe goes into a few impromptu rhumba steps.*)

MEN:

> You can dodge a stick or a stone,
> You can duck a punch when it's thrown,
> But you can't get away from a dumb tomato
> When she wants you for her own!

(Pancho plays a four-bar trumpet interlude and all the men do a few awkward versions of Latin steps.)

JOE:

> You may be a young and an innocent boy,
> Your chin grows only fuzz,
> But if a ripe tomato comes after you,
> You won't be as young as you wuz!

> You can dodge a bill when it's due,
> You can duck a flying lassoo,
> But you can't get away from a wild tomato
> When she throws herself at you.

(The refrain is repeated by the orchestra but is not sung by anyone. Instead the men all dance to it with Joe. They get Fauna to dance with them on occasion. Joe then goes into another verse.)

> You may be a good and respectable man,
> No cards, no gin, no rum—
> But if a wild tomato comes after you
> She will turn you into a bum.

MEN:

> You can dodge a bill when it's due,
> You can duck a flying lassoo—

JOE:

> But you can't get away from a ripe tomato
> When she throws a curve at you.

MEN:

> Man, you're through,
> There is nothing you can do
> When they throws their curves at you!

(*Pancho plays the trumpet again and the men go into a dance, getting more active and more extravagant in their illustrations of how they think tomatoes "throw curves" at them. Fauna, now armed with a bongo drum, begins to shout at the top of her voice.*)

FAUNA:

Babaloo! Babaloo! Babaloo! . . .

> I have heard you say
> How tomatoes are the ruin of man,
> But I ain't seen the day or the night
> When a woman made a pass at a man,
> And the man put up a fight.

> You can't catch a fish without a worm for bait,
> You can't catch a worm if you get up too late,

You can't plug a duck unless you sit and wait
And snarin' a bear is no snap.
The zebra is hard to catch and hard to tame.
Among all the animals we call wild game,
A man is the only one that you can name
Who tries to be caught in a trap!
You hunt him at nightfall.
He's easily thrown.
He's gotta go rovin',
He can't be alone.
He looks out the window when the moon is high,
He looks in the lookin' glass and ties his tie,
Decides he's a fascinatin' type of guy
And goes out and looks for a trap
    To be caught in,
He goes out and looks for the trap!

The zebra is hard to catch and hard to tame,
Among all the animals we call wild game,
There ain't any animals that you can name,
As wild and as dumb as a man.
You hunt him at nightfall.
He's easy to get.
If you are a female
He'll fall in your net.
He walks into trouble with a hopeful eye,
A pigeon who wants to be a pigeon pie,
A fish who is feelin' in the mood to fry,

He goes out and looks for a pan
    To be fried in!
He goes out and looks for the pan!

(*The men dance with her, get a careful grip on her, and hoist her high above their shoulders.*)

act one: scene 4

Cannery Row, a few days later, on a Sweet Thursday.

Suzy is walking slowly, gingerly carrying a fancy-looking cake. Offstage behind her we hear a wolf whistle. She stops and turns.

SUZY: Somebody want a cake in his kisser?

MAC (*entering with Hazel*): Hold it, Suzy. It was only me makin' like a wolf.

HAZEL: Whatcha doin' with the cake?

SUZY: Takin' it over to Doc. (*Catching herself up suddenly*) Fauna told me to.
(*She turns abruptly and goes on her way. The boys turn and look after her.*)

HAZEL: How do you figger that kid, Mac?

MAC: She's what I call a "special." Won't play no rules. She'd take a punch at Rocky Marciano if she didn't like what he said. Got a quality somethin' like Doc.

HAZEL (*outraged*): Like Doc!

MAC: Well, you know—*somethin'* like.

HAZEL: Talkin' of Doc—this idea you got about the raffle, I don't understand how—

MAC (*looking off, speaking quietly and quickly*): Just a minute, Hazel. Here comes the Mexican. If you listen while I tell him about the raffle, you'll get the whole thing.

HAZEL: You gonna tell the Mexican?

MAC: I *got* to tell him. How can we raffle off the Flophouse if he knows he owns it?

HAZEL: But he *don't* know . . . does he?

MAC (*lowering his voice to a hoarse whisper*): That's what I got to find out right now. That's the whole idea, ain't it? (*Mac puts on a warm smile as Joe enters.*)
Hiya, Joe?

JOE (*without enthusiasm*): Hi.

HAZEL (*angrily, as Joe passes them*): Hi, yerself! (*Mac gives Hazel a rib-breaking dig with his elbow and Hazel is knocked out of breath for a while.*)

MAC (*in a soft, warm, friendly voice*): Er—Joe, could I talk to you a minute?

JOE: I am in kind of a hurry.

MAC: Joe, you ain't lived here long . . . Joe . . . but you got a lot of good friends. (*Joe's eyelids lower sleepily, but he is as alert as a radar screen.*)
I and the boys want to ask your advice.

JOE: Yeh?

MAC: You see. For years Doc's took care of us—get sick he cures us, get broke he's there with a buck.

JOE: Everybody says the same.

HAZEL (*expressively*): Damn right they do!

(*Mac darts a warning look at him, then turns back to Joe.*)

MAC: That's right. Now Doc needs help. He can't crack them octopusses without he gets a big bastard of a microscope. Cost about three hundred bucks.

JOE (*relieved that it is so simple a hustle*): If you pass the hat I'll put in ten bucks.

MAC: I and the boys don't want your ten bucks. We want your advice.

JOE (*worried again*): I would rather just give you the ten bucks.

MAC: We got something and we want to raffle it. Then we want to take the raffle money and buy the microscope for Doc.

JOE: What you goin' to raffle?
(*Here it comes! The big test. Mac swallows and then comes out with it.*)

MAC: We want to raffle—(*he looks very closely at Joe*) the Palace Flophouse—our home—*the only thing we boys own*!

JOE: Have you decided who's going to win the raffle?
(*Pause. Mac and Hazel stand still and tense.*)

MAC: Well, we got to have some place to live, don't we? So we'll sell Doc a ticket, and we'll rig the raffle so he wins.

HAZEL: Now I get it!
(*Mac gives him another poke in ribs.*)

JOE: I don't.

MAC: Doc gets his microscope with the four hundred we make from the raffle, don't he?
(*Joe nods.*)

And we go right on habiting in the Palace Flophouse, only it's Doc's—

JOE: Suppose he sells it?

MAC: Doc? Not a chance! He wouldn't never put us out in the street.

(*A smile spreads over Joe's face.*)

JOE: Mac, I guess I never give you proper credit. You're smart. You got the raffle tickets?

MAC: We made 'em up last night. (*Takes bunch out of his pocket.*)

JOE: How much apiece?

MAC: Says right on them. Two bucks.

JOE: I could unload nearly fifty. (*Taking some tickets from Mac*) What the customers don't buy I'll sell to the wetbacks.

MAC: Gee, Joe, the boys'll sure be grateful for the attitude you're takin' about this.

JOE: Don't mention it. See you later. (*He starts out, then turns.*)

You know what I thought at first? I thought you was tryin' to hustle me.

(*He laughs and Mac laughs. Hazel, too, but just a little too loudly. Music starts. Joe exits. Mac and Hazel show great relief. Alec enters at right; George enters at left. They all look off left to be sure Joe is out of earshot.*)

HAZEL (*in a dramatic whisper*): He don't know he owns the Flophouse!

GEORGE: You sure?

MAC: He bought five raffle tickets and he's goin' to sell fifty more!

ALEC (*shouting*): Whoopee!

(*They shush him. Then softly they pick up the refrain of "Lopsided Bus," singing it with restrained gaiety, controlling their volume but giving away their happiness and relief in their voices and faces. With hands on one another's shoulders they dance off the stage.*)

act one: scene 5

The Western Biological Laboratory, immediately following previous scene.

Doc is sitting at his table working. Beside the small aquarium on the table are sheafs of notes, a long yellow pad, and four or five pencils.

DOC (*reading his notes*): "Observed reactions when stimulated with a glass needle. Color change; flickering motion of tentacle ends. Increased pulsing."

SUZY (*knocking on the door and entering with cake*): Can I come in?

DOC: Sure! What you got there, Suzy?

SUZY: A cake. Fauna sent it over to you.

DOC: I wonder why.

SUZY: She thought you'd like it, I guess.

DOC: Hmm. Will you have a piece with me, Suzy?

SUZY: Sure. (*She goes to a drawer for a knife.*)

DOC: I see you know where the knives are kept.

    (*Suzy stops short in the middle of the action like a criminal who has been caught. Doc continues to speak as he smiles at her.*)

Know what happened while I was at the tide pool yesterday? A leprechaun got in here and did a little housecleaning. I found my scalpels and forceps in the drawer with the forks and spoons.

SUZY: Yeh?

DOC: Then, in the spice cabinet I found a two-ounce jar of ozmic acid—only about enough to *kill* a couple of regiments.

SUZY: What do you know!

DOC: Reason I know it was a leprechaun—I found some wonderful Irish stew cooking slowly on the stove.

SUZY (*dropping all pretense*): Did you like it?

DOC: I sure did! Thanks, Suzy.

SUZY: Want to try the cake now? (*She goes over toward the cake.*)

DOC: Guess we might as well. Have you any idea what Fauna wants to get out of me?

SUZY (*Holding the knife above the cake without moving it, and suddenly bridling*): What makes you think she wants to get somethin' out of you?

DOC: Why else did she send me this cake out of a clear sky?

SUZY: Couldn't somebody give you a cake without wantin' somethin'? Couldn't it just be because—she likes you? (*Putting the knife down*) You eat it yourself. I ain't stayin'. (*She starts to go. As she crosses to the door she continues to rant*) You stay here by yourself and make out you're writin' a big damn highfalutin paper!

DOC: What do you mean by that?

SUZY (*stopping at the door*): Everybody in Cannery Row is laughing behind your back because everybody knows you won't ever write that paper. You're just sittin' in here like a kid playin' wishing games.

DOC: Suzy! What else are they saying?

SUZY: They all say what a hell of a guy you used to be! *Used to be—get it?*

(*She slams the door. Outside the door she gets in a panic. She turns back to the door but hasn't the nerve to open it again. She exits.*)

DOC (*taking up his notes with a sigh, reading*): "Possible release of something like adrenalin"—I think. But no way to prove it, no way to see it. (*Throwing his notes down*) No damned adequate microscope! . . . Is it the microscope? Is that the whole trouble, or has Suzy got you sized up right? Are you only like a kid playing wishing games? That'd be a good joke . . . but you wouldn't laugh. You can't laugh at your-self any more the way you used to.

(*He starts to sing softly*)

You've changed, Bub,

You've changed a lot—

And the gang you used to go with all concur.

You've changed, Bub,

You're not yourself—

If this *is* yourself, you're not the man you were!

(*Music continues under dialogue.*)

Why all of a sudden is it no fun to do the things I used to like doing? I used to putter around here, read a book, play phonograph records, every day ended with a night and I was satisfied. People used to like me. (*He smiles.*) I used to like myself.

(*He resumes singing*)

The man I used to be,
A happy man was he,
And aimless as a leaf in a gale.
Whatever has become
Of that light-hearted bum
Who thought he had the world by the tail?
The man I used to be—
His life was gay and free
And aimless as a cloud in the sky.
He thought he knew the game,
Then along came a dame
Who turned him into some other guy.
I've got ambition, now.
I've got a mission, now.
I aim to reach the top of the tree.
That other fly-by-night

Who flew so high by night,
Has vanished like a sail on the sea,
And I'll never find that easy-living,
    easy-taking, easy-giving fellow that I used to call me—
You can never find the man you used to be.

(*Dance interlude: Doc's "former self" enters and flits about the stage easily and gracefully to contrast with the worried "self" who sings the song.*)

The man I used to be,
Would go to sleep at three
Or four a.m. or seven or nine,
And when his weary head
Wasn't near any bed
A table or a chair would be fine!
A man without a goal,
A sort of friendly soul,
He liked to play the role of a host
To any thirsty pal
Or a casual gal
Who'd stay to cook his coffee and toast.
He was a ne'er do well
Who wouldn't dare do well,
He never saw the top of a tree,
But kind of sad I was
To see the cad I was
Dissolving like a sail on the sea,

And I'll never find that fatalistic,
   free-and-easy egotistic optimist who used to be me—

(There is a musical interlude now during which Doc attempts to dance as gracefully as we have seen his old self do a few minutes before. He gives up after tripping and proving to himself that he is just not as nimble as he was.)

You can never find the man you used to be.

(There is a knock on the door and then Fauna comes in.)

DOC: Hello, Fauna.

FAUNA: I hope I'm not interruptin' you right in the middle of somethin'.

DOC: No, I wasn't getting anywhere. . . . Thanks for the cake.

FAUNA: You was right, what you told Suzy about me sendin' the cake because I wanted somethin'. Only I couldn't tell *her* what it was.

DOC *(smiling)*: Well? What was it?

FAUNA: You must get sick of everybody wantin' somethin' from you.

DOC: I'd be sicker if they didn't. What can I do, Fauna?

FAUNA: I got the Coyote Club comin' over from Salinas tonight. They took the whole house over.

DOC: They do that every year, don't they?

FAUNA: Yeh. This year they're makin' it a memorial meeting for dead members.

DOC: Kind of a rough crowd as I remember.

FAUNA: Well, that's how you can do me the favor. You see, I don't want Suzy around. She won't do the party no good. Tell you the truth, she's a complete bust over there. No use kidding myself.

DOC: Where do I come in?

(*Pause.*)

FAUNA: Lemme ask you somethin'. When you're makin' a play for one of them babes, them amateurs that come in here and leave their fancy automobiles outside, know what I mean?

(*Doc nods.*)

Well, ain't it right you got to do quite a lot of talkin' before you make the sack, ain't that right?

(*Doc smiles and nods, "Right."*)

Well, do you always mean every word you say to them?

DOC: Why—I guess right at the moment I do.

FAUNA: But afterward?

DOC: Afterward, if I were to think about it—

FAUNA: That's what I mean. So if you happen to tell a little baloney, you don't blow your brains out.

(*Pause.*)

DOC: What do you want me to do, Fauna?

FAUNA: I want you to help me get this kid Suzy off my neck. (*Doc frowns. Then he turns on a tighter, more incredulous frown. In fact, he "makes a face" at Fauna.*)

DOC: Then she'd be on *my* neck.

FAUNA: You don't marry them others.

DOC: No, I don't. (*He thinks this over.*)

FAUNA: Take a whang at her, will you, Doc?
(*Doc shakes his head and opens his mouth to say "No," but Fauna doesn't give him the chance.*)
I'll give you odds, three to one, if you do make a play for Suzy—like she was a lady—you won't get her!
DOC: That's an interesting idea.
FAUNA: It's a *hell* of an interestin' idea! (*She looks out of the window thoughtfully.*) By the way, Doc, what day was you born?
DOC: July fourth, 1920.
FAUNA: The fourth of July. Did you notice what a beautiful day it is today, Doc?
DOC: Yes, I noticed.
FAUNA (*walking over to him and looking at him hard*): Will you do it?
DOC: No.
FAUNA: Aw, Doc—
DOC: I'll tell you what I *will* do. I'll take her off your hands for tonight. I'll ask her out to dinner. That'll solve your problem for one night anyway.
FAUNA: Will you do that, Doc? That's great! I'll tell her.
DOC: No. Let me invite her. You want me to treat her like a lady, don't you?
FAUNA: You're a swell guy, Doc.
DOC: You're kinda cute yourself.
(*He gives her a kiss.*)
FAUNA (*looking out again*): Yes, sir. One gorgeous day, that's

what it is. Ain't it funny about days? Like today everything
falls into place.
(*She sings*)

When the sun flew in my window
And crept in bed with me,
I knew that this would be
A Sweet Thursday.
When the wind got confidential
And whispered through a tree,
I knew that this would be
A Sweet Thursday.

My head was up in the clouds,
My heart was flapping its wings.
I looked at the sky
And wanted to try
To do impossible things.

What a day it's been for dreaming,
My dreams have all come true,

And if one I kept for you
Turns out to be right,
It's going to be a Sweet Thursday Night for me!
It's going to be a Sweet Thursday Night!

(She goes out into the street, leaving Doc scratching his head in puzzlement over her inordinate gaiety. The lights dim. The music of the song continues.)

act one: scene 6

Cannery Row

Out in the street Fauna walks along in happy contemplation, continuing her song.

FAUNA (*singing*):
> A good kind of confident feeling
> Has followed me all day long.
> My luck was in,
> I played to win—
> I knew I couldn't go wrong.
>
> A bright red geranium told me,
> Today was my day for fun.
> A katydid
> Said, "Take it, kid,
> You better take it and run!"
>
> Some shirts hanging up on a clothes line
> Kept waving their tails my way—
> "Hiya, Fauna? Hiya, babe?
> Ain't this a doll of a day?"

(*Johnny and Pedro enter and wave to Fauna.*)

BOYS: Hi, Fauna.

FAUNA: Hi, boys.

(*The two boys join Fauna on either side and dance with her as she sings.*)

Ain't this a doll of day?

When the sun flew in my window
And crept in bed with me,
I knew that this would be
A sweet Thursday.
When the wind got confidential
And whispered through a tree,
I knew that this would be
A Sweet Thursday.
My head was up in the clouds,
My heart was flapping its wings.
I looked at the sky
And wanted to try
To do impossible things.
What a day it's been for dreaming,
My dreams have all come true,
And if one for Doc and Sue
Turns out to be right,
It's going to be a Sweet Thursday Night for me!
It's going to be a sweet Thursday night!

(*She exits with an exultant strut.*)

act one: scene 7

A room in the Bear Flag Cafe.

It is a pleasant room with deep chairs and couches covered with bright flower-littered chintz. On a card table is a parcheesi board and Emma and Mabel are playing. Agnes is seated at the table, Beulah standing beside it. Marjorie is putting polish on her toenails. Suzy is gazing out a window, which faces the audience.

EMMA: Natural! Read 'em, suckers!

BEULAH: What do you mean "natural"?

EMMA: Whatsa matter—you unliterated? Add 'em—four and three.

AGNES (*standing*): I had enough. Any broad that would cheat at parcheesi don't deserve to work in a nice place like this! (*She crosses to get a cigarette on the other side of the room.*)

MARJORIE: Like this color?

AGNES: It's nice. Looks like you was rotting! (*coming down, looking out window with Suzy*) What do you see out the window that you like so much better than us?

SUZY: I was looking at that old boiler in the lot out there.

AGNES (*crossing back to the card table*): Oh!

SUZY: Fauna told me people lived in it once. Was she kiddin' me?

MARJORIE: No. I knew them—Mr. and Mrs. Molloy. They had it fixed up nice. Awning out front, oriental rug. Once you got inside through the fire door, it was real nice.

SUZY: Imagine! Livin' in a boiler.

MARJORIE (*rising*): I think I'll do my fingernails now.

AGNES: You're sure puttin' on the warpaint for those Coyotes.

SUZY: What kind of fellers are they?

AGNES: The most boring bunch of bastards I ever met in my life.

FAUNA (*entering with horoscope book*): Hello, girls!

GIRLS: Hi, Fauna.

FAUNA: Suzy, what's your birthday?

SUZY: February twenty-third.

FAUNA (*looking in her book to make sure*): February twenty-third. That's Pisces! (*To Suzy*) You're fish.

SUZY: I don't even like fish. I break out if I look at it.

FAUNA (*studying the book and mumbling*): Maybe I'll tell you who you're goin' to marry.

SUZY (*crosses to downstage chair at table and sits*): Who wants to get married?

FAUNA (*ignoring Suzy, continuing to calculate*): You know what I always wanted? (*She turns away from Suzy very deliberately and addresses the other girls.*) I always wanted one of our girls to marry Doc.

(*Suzy snorts, walks upstage, and looks out the window.*)

I been savin' him for somebody. We ain't never had a girl here I'd pick out for him.

SUZY: That guy don't want any wife. He's too mean.

FAUNA: Men don't know what they want. Why should any guys in their right mind want to get married? But they do.

SUZY: Guess they marry because they fall for somebody.

FAUNA: And it's ninety to one they fall for the wrong one! That's why it's better for somebody to make up their mind for them.

SUZY: How do you mean?

FAUNA: A guy who picks out a dame for himself is in love with something in himself that hasn't got nothin' to do with the dame. She looks like his mother, or she's dark and he's scared of blondes. The best marriages are the ones pulled off by someone that's smart—like me. Now, I think you'd be good for Doc.

SUZY: Me! Fauna, you're nuts! (*She walks away and turns.*) Why do you think I'd be good for Doc?

FAUNA (*pointing to her book*): Because you're fish and Doc's a crab, born on July fourth. That means you'd go great together. . . . You want I should try to land him?

SUZY: I wouldn't sandbag a guy.

FAUNA: Everybody sandbags everybody!

(*There is a knock on the door.*)

Come in!

(*Mac enters.*)

Oh, hello, Mac. I got your money. We sold ten tickets for your raffle. (*She gives him the money.*)

MAC: Thanks. What I come for is to tell you we're going to give a *fancy dress party* the night we draw the numbers.
(*The girls respond enthusiastically to this announcement.*)
It's goin' to be a Wallager. I can't wait to see Doc's face when he wins.

FAUNA: How you goin' to explain it to him when he wins and he didn't buy no ticket?

MAC: We'll say a friend did it and don't want his name mentioned.
(*The phone rings. Fauna immediately starts whistling "Sweet Thursday," looking pointedly at Suzy. Marjorie answers the phone.*)

MARJORIE: . . . Just a minute. For you, Suzy.
(*Suzy, surprised and awed and vaguely frightened, goes to the phone. Fauna signals all the other girls to scram, which they do.*)

SUZY (*in phone*): Hello . . . I . . . I'll call you back. (*She hangs up the receiver slowly and turns to look at Fauna.*)
Doc wants me to go out to dinner with him.
(*Pause. Mac dashes out the door. This is not the kind of news you can keep from your friends.*)

FAUNA: You got any gloves?

SUZY: No.

FAUNA: I'll lend you some. Always wear clean gloves, take care of your shoes, and keep your stocking seams straight. If you do that you can get away with murder.
(*Suzy seems too stunned to talk.*)

And remember one thing when you're out in public—do everything slow. Walk slow. (*She walks grandly off but continues to talk from her room.*) Sit down slow. Lift your glass to your lips and drink slow. Makes you look like you're dignified, get it?

(*Meanwhile Suzy has walked back to the phone and is looking at it indecisively. Fauna comes out of her room with armament.*)

You can hang these bo'martens over your shoulder, and if you lose them I'll cut your tripes out.

(*Suzy walks over toward Fauna, fright in her eyes, her mouth turned down in blind panic.*)

What the hell's the matter with you?

SUZY: Call him up and tell him I'm sick. I ain't goin'.

FAUNA: The hell you ain't goin'.

SUZY: I ain't no good, Fauna. You been nice, but you're just wastin' your time. I'm scared.

FAUNA: 'Course you're scared. There ain't never been a dame went out first time with a guy she liked that wasn't scared.

SUZY: He'll say somethin' I don't understand, and I'll open my yap and make a fool of myself.

FAUNA: Don't open it. Not until you thought three times about what you're goin' to say. You say to yourself: "Think!"

(*There is a "plink" in the orchestra.*)

"Think!"

(*Another "plink" in the orchestra.*)

And when you thunk—then you talk—or you decide not to talk. Get it?

SUZY (*hoarsely, still in a panic*): Yeh, I get it.

FAUNA: Now I want you should say after me: "I'm Suzy and nobody else."

SUZY (*mechanically*): I'm Suzy and nobody else.

FAUNA: "I'm a good thing."

(*Pause.*)

SUZY: I ain't.

FAUNA: The hell you ain't! (*Grabbing Suzy's shoulders*) Now listen! I want you to say everything I say . . .

(*Singing*)

I got eyes that can see pretty sunsets—

SUZY (*singing*):

I got eyes that can see pretty sunsets.

(*The rest of the scene is sung, except when otherwise indicated.*)

FAUNA:

And pretty dresses in store winders—

SUZY:

And pretty dresses in store winders.

FAUNA:

    And I got ears that can hear music—

SUZY:

    And I got ears that can hear music.

FAUNA:

    And the sound of waves on a beach—

SUZY:

    And the sound of waves on a beach.

FAUNA:

    I got a nose that can smell flowers—

SUZY:

    I got a nose that can smell flowers.

FAUNA:

    And food cookin' on a stove—

SUZY:

    And food cookin' on a stove.

FAUNA:

    And I got two feet that can take me
        Anywhere I want to go—

SUZY:

    And I got two feet that can take me
        Anywhere I want to go.

FAUNA:

    And I can walk and run and climb
        and swim in the sea—

SUZY:

    And I can walk and run and climb
        and swim in the sea.

FAUNA:
And if I am somethin' that can do all this,
Why should I
Be ashamed to be me?

SUZY:
And if I am somethin' that can do all this,
Why should I
Be ashamed to be me?

(*Suzy's voice is gaining confidence. The music becomes sweeter, tenderer.*)

FAUNA (*speaking very earnestly, pleading*): Listen to me, honey . . .
(*Singing*)
Suzy is a good thing,
This I know is true.
Suzy is a good thing.
She may make mistakes
As other people do—
Everybody makes a few.
Suzy's eyes are searching eyes,
The world they seek is new.
Suzy looks for love
As other people do.
Suzy will find her love, too . . .
Someone is looking for Sue.
(*Pause.*)
Tonight you're goin' out with a man—

SUZY (*taking over*):
> With a man who asked me to go!

FAUNA:
> Right!

SUZY:
> And I ain't scared o' sayin' anythin' wrong
> 'Cause I won't say only what I know!

FAUNA:
> Good!

SUZY:
> I'm goin' out to eat tonight.
> A feller is takin' me there,
> I'll hold my hand on his arm good and tight
> And I'll hold my chin in the air
> (*her brow darkens*)
> And if anyone tries to make a crack—
> (*catching Fauna's warning eye, and hearing a "plink" in the orchestra*)
> I'll look like I don't care.
> Because I'm Suzy!
> Suzy is a good thing!

FAUNA:
> This I know is true!

BOTH:
> Suzy is a good thing.
> She may make mistakes
> As other people do—
> Everybody makes a few.

FAUNA:

> Suzy's eyes are searching eyes,
> The world they seek is new.

SUZY:

> Suzy looks for love
> As other people do.

BOTH:

> Suzy will find her love, too!
> Someone is looking for Sue.

act one: scene 8

Cannery Row, the same evening.

The street is quickly filled up with all the people of Cannery Row. Some bring on boxes to stand on as though to watch a parade.

GIRL (*to Joe*): Did you hear?

JOE: What do you think we're here for?

GIRL: Just asking. (*To Agnes*) Did you hear?

AGNES: What do you think we are doing here?

GIRL: Just asking.

AGNES: What a dumb broad!

GIRL (*starting to ask the same question of another girl in the crowd*) Did you hear?

(*Mac enters right.*)

MAC: I peeked in the window—he's putting on a necktie!

(*George rushes on, left.*)

GEORGE: Quiet! He's coming!

(*Doc enters.*)

HAZEL (*as Doc passes him*): Hi, Doc. What's the idea of the necktie?

DOC: Oh, just thought I'd wear one.

(*He exits.*)

JOHNNY (*stepping from behind crowd*): Hey, what's going on here?

(*He is pushed back by the crowd. All eyes turn in the direction taken by Doc. He is heard knocking on the door of the Bear Flag Cafe. There is general excitement before Doc and Suzy enter. A girl sneezes and some in the crowd whisper "God bless you!" The crowd whispers along the line, as Suzy apparently comes out of the door, "She's out." Doc and Suzy enter. They walk together, looking straight ahead of them. As they pass, a girl in the crowd sighs romantically; she is quickly shushed by those around her. The two little boys, Johnny and Pedro, follow Doc and Suzy, imitating their walk. They are quickly pushed into the background by the crowd. Doc and Suzy exit, and the crowd picks up the refrain of "Sweet Thursday." The denizens of Cannery Row are all very, very happy.*)

act one: scene 9

Sonny Boy's Pier Restaurant.

A "shore-dinner place" on the beach. Dim lamps, glasses filled with a bouquet of breadsticks, on each table.

On the backdrop is the beach and sky.

The stage lighting is dull, but suddenly the moon falls on the beach. The table lights grow more beautifully mellow and the whole scene takes on a light of romantic radiance as Suzy and Doc enter. The eyes of all are on them, as they are on any newly arrived couple. Suzy feels the looks and holds her head up proudly as she walks in front of Doc. They are both led to their table by Sonny Boy, who gives Doc the respectful attention that distinguished and well-known patrons deserve. At the table, Suzy starts to sit down, but she stops and thinks (and there is a "plink" in the orchestra). Doc is holding a chair for her. She leaves the chair she was about to sit in, walks over to the other chair, and lets Doc slip it under her as she sits at the table. Suzy looks up at him and smiles.

SUZY: Thank you.

SONNY BOY (*to Doc*): Good you telephoned. I had trouble getting pompano, but I got it. (*Pointing to the dishes in front of them*) There is your cracked crab. Your wine is cooling. How about a cocktail?

DOC: Let's see, Sonny Boy, what was that thing you gave me the last time I was here?

SONNY BOY: A cocktail? (*Remembering*) Oh. The Webster F. Street Layaway Plan. A little invention of mine. A martini with chartreuse instead of vermouth.

DOC: Very effective, as I remember it. Two doubles.

SONNY BOY: Coming right up.

(*He leaves them. Doc and Suzy are a little nervous and tentative, left alone with each other. There is a rather long pause, which Doc breaks.*)

DOC: I'm very fond of cracked crab.

SUZY (*dubiously nibbling on a piece*): Yeh.

DOC: How are *you* on shellfish?

SUZY: Great.

(*Suzy laughs. Doc's hand goes to his necktie and he twitches his neck inside his collar.*)

Collar tight?

DOC: No, I'm just not used to wearing a necktie.

SUZY: Take it off.

DOC: No, I'll keep it on.

SUZY: Why did you wear a tie tonight anyway?

(*Pause.*)

DOC: I just thought I'd wear one.

SUZY (*about to make fun of the idea*): Well, why the hell— (*She stops and thinks. There is a "plink" in the orchestra, and then she smiles at him.*)
Thank you. It looks nice.
(*Doc nods a grave acknowledgment. A waiter serves them each a cocktail in a large double glass and disappears. Suzy's hand moves out fast toward the glass. She starts to lift it, quickly. There is a "plink" in the orchestra. She stops, holding it an inch above the table, remembering Fauna's advice to "take it slow." Doc lifts his glass and then Suzy lifts hers, but very slowly. He looks at her over his glass and holds it up to be clinked. She clinks her glass with his—very slowly! Then she slowly puts it to her lips, takes a drink, and now unfortunately all the dignity of slowness leaves her. Quickly she puts the glass down and gasps out a choking cough. Doc smiles at her.*)

SUZY: I was watching its right hand and walked into a left hook. (*Catching herself up*) I said that without thinking.

DOC: It was fine. Say some more without thinking.

SUZY: Fauna says I should always think before I talk.

DOC: Does Fauna always think before she talks?

SUZY (*thinking it over*): I . . . don't suppose she does.
(*Doc offers her a cigarette, which she takes.*)
Otherwise she wouldn't of asked me to live with her. I bet she's sorry she didn't think *that* over first.

DOC (*passing her a light*): Are *you*?

SUZY (*leaning forward very slowly to take the light*): Sorry?

No. . . . Why should I be sorry? I was flat on my—
(*"Plink!"*)
I don't know what I'd of done without Fauna. I love Fauna.
DOC: I guess I do too.
(*They drink again.*)
SUZY: I feel warm inside. Do I look warm outside?
DOC: You look pretty.
SUZY (*disdainfully*): Ah—
(*"Plink!"*)
Thank you.
(*The waiter arrives with two orders of pompano.*)
DOC: Like pompano?
SUZY: It's fish, ain't it?
DOC: That's right!
SUZY: Love it!
(*Doc starts to eat; Suzy starts everything a little later and imitates him. Meanwhile the waiter has brought some white wine, which they drink. At this point, Esteban, off-stage, begins to sing softly, in Spanish.*)
DOC: Do you like that wine?
SUZY: Fine. What kind is it?
DOC: It's an Alsatian wine.
SUZY: Like where the dogs come from?
DOC: Same place.
SUZY: Europe some place, huh?
DOC: That's right.
SUZY: It's good. Soft and smooth. Kinda like layin' on a cushion after that cocktail.

DOC (*indicating a vase of iris in the middle of the table*):
Waiter, can we have these flowers removed? (*Catching a
look on Suzy's face, he explains*) So we can see each other.

SUZY: Couldn't we keep 'em on the table and put 'em to one
side? So we could see each other and still have the flowers?
(*The waiter carries out her suggestion.*)

DOC: You like flowers?

SUZY: I like 'em on a dinner table—you know why?

DOC: No, why?

SUZY: Because it's the first time I ever eat with flowers on the
table.
(*Doc raises his glass again to her, and she raises hers, and
they drink. There is a glow over the table now. Doc is en-
chanted with her. She puts down her glass slowly now and
looks back at him. Esteban, who has come onto the stage
and is singing to people at the other tables, now observes
this pair of lovers and walks over to them, directing his song
at them. Doc smiles at him, and then Suzy smiles at him.
He continues to sing to them, making his exit at the end of
the refrain. Offstage he continues to play his guitar, but he
is no longer singing.*)

DOC: Nice voice.

SUZY: Pretty melody . . . wish I knew what the words
meant. . . . Do *you* know what they mean?
(*Doc nods. Suzy asks shyly*)
Would you say them for me?

DOC (*feeling instinctively that he is on dangerous ground*):
Well, it's about two people . . .

SUZY: You know, that's just what I figgered. Ain't that funny?
And I don't know a word of Mexican!
*(Doc laughs and lights Suzy's cigarette. The music now is
approaching the beginning of the refrain, and Doc sings)*

DOC:

You start to light
Her cigarette
And all at once
You love her.
You've scarcely talked,
You've scarcely met,
But all at once
You love her.
You like her eyes,
You tell her so.
She thinks you're wise
And clever.
You kiss good night
And then you know
You'll kiss good night
Forever!

You wonder where
Your heart can go—
Then all at once you know.
(*The end of the number finds them looking into each other's eyes.*)

SUZY: Hey, Doc, will you some time teach me about the stuff you got in your place?

DOC: Sure I will.

(*The waiter has come behind the table and taken the champagne bottle out of the bucket and now starts to open it.*)
You know, out in the sand dunes there, there are little valleys covered with pines. Some time—when you can—let's take meat and things out there and cook our supper. It's very nice.

SUZY: It sounds nice.

(*They gaze at each other. There is a sudden pop of a cork and Suzy jumps.*)
What the hell was that?

WAITER: Sorry, madame.

SUZY: Oh, the cork, huh?

(*The waiter starts to pour the wine. Suzy picks up the cork from the table, puts it in her bag. The champagne is poured. They drink to each other.*)
You know that place you said, out in the sand dunes?

DOC: Yes.

SUZY: Could we look at it?

DOC: Whenever you want.

SUZY: On our way home?

DOC: You'll mess your shoes.

SUZY: I know.

DOC: You could take them off.

SUZY: I will.

(*She picks up refrain of music which has been playing during their dialogue*)

You kiss good night

And then you know

You'll kiss good night

Forever.

DOC AND SUZY:

You wonder where your heart can go

And all at once you know.

(*The curtain falls slowly.*)

ACT TWO

act two: scene 1

A room in the Bear Flag Cafe, the following morning.

*Fauna and the girls are draped around the stage in various atti-
tudes of female repose, relaxing on the morning after a strenu-
ous night.*

MARJORIE (*entering right*): Let me tell you something, if
   that Coyote Club comes here to hold another Memorial
   Meeting for dead members, I'm leaving!
AGNES: Don't worry, the way they looked last night it won't
   be no time at all before they run out of live members. Even
   the guy who left his Yo Yo here didn't have a very good
   time.
FAUNA: Did any of you get a chance to talk to Suzy when she
   come in last night?
AGNES: No. She come in long after we got to sleep.
EMMA: I wonder how Suzy and Doc—(*she pauses and holds
   her head as though even speaking is painful*) made out.
MABEL: I bet they give in to each other.
FAUNA (*beaming as she starts to take a large card out of a large*

envelope): I got a surprise for you dames. Our Christmas card is ready!

MARJORIE: Christmas card! It's only July!

FAUNA: You gotta order them now if you want a good job. (*She holds up a very large card for the girls to see, and they all cluster around her and coo with delight.*)

MARJORIE: Ain't that pretty!

EMMA: Look, a picture of the house!

FAUNA: Got a refined, homelike feelin', huh? Now look inside. (*She opens the folder.*)

MARJORIE: Poetry!

FAUNA: Got a friend of mine in Frisco to write it for me. It come out real pretty.

(*She starts to sing*)

"Merry Christmas from me and the family,
Remember if ever you're blue,
This little frame house on the corner
Will always be open to you.

"The happiest house on the block
Is quietly sleeping all day,
But after eleven

Our little blue heaven
Is friendly and foolish and gay.
The roses that grow round our door
Will welcome you in when you knock.
You'll meet everyone in
The town having fun in
The happiest house on the block."

MARJORIE:

What a beautiful holiday greeting!

MABEL:

Look at Santa Claus blowin' a kiss!

EMMA:

It makes a girl proud to be part of
An organization like this.

FAUNA:

The happiest house on the block,
Where nothing's too good for a guest.

GIRLS:

Our parlor is cheery,
There's rest for the weary,
The weary who don't want to rest!

FAUNA:

A home for the brave and the free,
Where nobody punches a clock—

GIRLS:

Alone, on that basis,
Our own little place is
The happiest house on the block.

FAUNA:

There's a friend who drops in very often.
He is kind of mixed up in his life.
He longs for a home and a woman
Whenever he's home with his wife.

(*In the next refrain Fauna hums an obbligato while the girls sing the melody.*)

GIRLS:

The happiest house on the block
Is quietly sleeping all day,
But after eleven
Our little blue heaven
Is friendly and foolish and gay.
The roses that grow round our door
Will welcome you in when you knock.
You'll meet everyone in
The town having fun in
The happiest house on the block.

FAUNA: Now I want you should all make a list of your friends so I know how many cards to order.
GIRLS (*their speeches overlapping*):
Gee, thanks, Fauna!
I guess you'll want their office addresses instead of their homes, huh?

Would you like the names of any organizations?
(*Suzy enters and immediately all the chattering stops. She brings a cup of coffee with her and sits at table right.*)

FAUNA: Well, good morning!

SUZY: Good mornin', everybody.

AGNES: Get Fauna to show you the Christmas card—

FAUNA: I'll show her later. I want you girls to scrounge around in your rooms for some clothes—you know, for the masquerade *tomorrow night*.
(*The girls, taking the hint, leave Fauna and Suzy alone. As soon as they have left, Fauna turns to Suzy.*)
Look at me.
(*Suzy raises her eyes. Fauna searches them for a moment.*)
You can look down now.
(*Suzy takes another sip of coffee.*)
Have a nice time?

SUZY: He didn't make a pass. We went out on the sand dunes and he didn't make a pass.

FAUNA: Did he talk nice?

SUZY: While we was havin' dinner—all of a sudden he says: "I'm lonely."

FAUNA: What are you goin' to do about it?

SUZY: About what?

FAUNA: About him being lonely.

SUZY (*depressed by the truth*): He don't need nobody like me. Know what I think? Doc needs a wife!

FAUNA: That's what I think! (*Studying Suzy*) You want I should try to land him for you?

SUZY (*getting up quickly and walking away*): Fauna, for a smart woman you sure can talk crazy!

FAUNA: What's crazy about it?

SUZY (*lashing out—against herself as much as at Fauna*): Don't he know I come off the road that night? Don't he know where I been ever since? I been here—with you—in this house!

(*Pause while Fauna looks at her with deep concern.*)

FAUNA: You sound like you love him . . . do you?

SUZY (*looking away*): All the time I'm with him I keep wishin' I was somebody else—somebody a hundred times better than me.

FAUNA (*doggedly*): You want I should try to land him for you?

SUZY: I wouldn't want to sandbag a guy like Doc.

FAUNA: Who's sandbaggin' anybody? If you love him like that, you got somethin' to give him. You ain't takin' anythin' away from him. (*starting to plan very efficiently*) Now you just leave everything to me. First we got this fancy-dress party comin' up tomorrow. We gotta make you look so pretty that he can't keep his hands off you.

SUZY: You're wastin' your time.

FAUNA: Then maybe at the party you could sing a little song or somethin'. Maybe that thing we hear on television all the time.

(*She sings*)

"Will you marry me?"

SUZY: What do you want me to do? Propose to him in front of everybody?

FAUNA: You don't have to sing it *at* him. Just sing it.

SUZY: I'd be too scared.

FAUNA: Scared of what, for cryin' out loud?

SUZY: Scared of *him*. Scared of what he thinks of me. Scared of what I know I am. If I tried to sing in front of him, my voice would dry up. My knees would knock together, and I'd make a holy show of myself.

FAUNA: I know this guy better than you do. You act like you're just as good as he is and you'll be all right. If you act like you think you're a no-good tramp, then that's what he'll think you are.

SUZY: That's all I am, is a tramp.

FAUNA: Did you act like one last night?
   (*Suzy shakes her head.*)
   Did he treat you like one?
   (*Suzy looks up at Fauna thoughtfully, impressed.*)
   Now I tell you what you do. You go upstairs and go back to bed and rest all day. I don't want him to see you till to-morrow night, and when he does see you I want you to be lookin' your best. I want you to walk into that party as if you owned the whole place and him with it.

SUZY (*weakly*): I'll make a holy show of myself.

FAUNA: Go upstairs to bed like I tell you.

SUZY: I got no chance.

FAUNA: If you got no chance, then you got nothin' to lose by doin' like I tell you. Now get! (*She gives Suzy a little slap.*)

SUZY (*whimpering as she goes off*): I'll make a holy show of myself.

(*The girls rush into the room.*)

MARJORIE: What happened?

MABEL: Did Suzy say anything about last night?

FAUNA: You know every damn word she said because you been listenin' at the door!

AGNES: What do you know about Doc not makin' a pass!

FAUNA: Didn't surprise me at all. I had it figured.

AGNES: Why do you want her to sing "Will You Marry Me?"

FAUNA: The word "marry" don't come natural to a man. You gotta keep throwin' it in front of him to kinda put it in his head. That's why a song like "Will you Marry Me?" comes in so handy for a girl. If men realized what these songwriters are doin' to them they'd throw them all in jail.

EMMA: Do you want us to lay all these things out so you can have a look at them?

FAUNA: Go ahead.

(*The girls start to lay their dresses out.*)

MARJORIE: I don't think any of this stuff is any good for a masquerade.

FAUNA: Mac and me have decided we ought to have a theme.

CHO CHO SEN: What's that?

FAUNA: It's like when all the costumes are part of a story.

EMMA: I know. It's like those fancy dress parties the swells give. Everybody comes togged out like a baby or somethin'.

MARJORIE: Or it may be seventeenth-century Venice.

FAUNA: Not around here it wouldn't be seventeenth-century

Venice. Gee, I wish we could get some idea that would be good for Suzy. How about givin' the party a name like "At the Court of the Fairy Queen"?

AGNES: That's lousy.

FAUNA: I didn't say it wasn't. I was just explainin' the idea. Some of these duds! If anybody went out just to mail a letter, she could get booked for vagrancy.

MARJORIE: That's what I say. They're too fancy for a fancy-dress party.

FAUNA: What you got there, Mabel?

MABEL (*apologetically*): A wedding dress. My grandma brought it from the old country. (*As she speaks she opens the brown paper parcel, sealed against air with strips of cellophane tape.*) She gave it to Mama and Mama gave it to me. (*She tears the paper open.*) We ain't none of us needed it.

(*She pulls out a wedding dress. Fauna takes it and looks at it, and then holds it against another girl to get a better look at it. She is very impressed and her mind is working a mile a minute.*)

FAUNA: Mabel! Would you loan this to Suzy?

MABEL: Well, that's just what I was thinkin'. If *you* thought it was a good idea.

FAUNA: I think it's a hell of an idea.

(*Mabel has taken out a silver wedding crown. She puts it on the head of the girl who is holding the dress.*)

MABEL: We could polish up this crown. It's kinda tarnished. Real silver!

(*The girls all gasp with admiration. Fauna studies the whole thing carefully.*)
We could tell her not to spill nothing on it. I wouldn't like it to spoil. (*Her hands go back into the paper package.*) There's a veil in the bag.

FAUNA: I don't know if we can get away with the veil.

MARJORIE: That's where your idea comes in. The theme. It's gotta be like this is a costoom that fits the party.

FAUNA: The thing is you can't let on she's supposed to be a bride, but she's got to be all in white.

CHO CHO SEN: How about Snow White?

(*Silence. They all look at her. Fauna is as one struck by lightning.*)

FAUNA (*rolling the phrase off her tongue grandly*): Snow White and the Seven Dwarfs!

AGNES (*the biggest girl there*): I ain't goin' to be no dwarf!

FAUNA: You don't have to. It don't make no difference what anybody else wears, only Suzy.

MAC (*entering and calling through the window*): Hey, Fauna, I got news! We sold three hundred and fifty-five bucks' worth of tickets for the raffle!

FAUNA: That enough to buy the microscope?

MAC: More than enough.

FAUNA: Doc'll be tickled!

MAC: I hope so. He's in an awful mood right now.

FAUNA (*her face lighting up as if this was the best news she has ever heard*): He is?

MAC: I seen him walkin' up and down on the beach all alone.
I waved to him but he hardly took no notice of me.

FAUNA (*happily*): You don't say!

MAC: Do you think anything happened between him and
that dame he took out last night?

FAUNA: Could be! Could be! Now let me tell you *my* news.
We thought of a theme for the party.

MAC: Give it to me slow.

FAUNA: Snow White and the Seven Dwarfs!

MAC: Hey, that's good! We could have a pageant! You might
be the head witch!

FAUNA: What the hell do you mean by that?

MAC: And then you turn out to be Snow White's fairy godmother, see?

FAUNA: Mac, that's great! I could wear my evening dress with
the white sequins.

MAC: Say, this is going to be a Tom Wallager of a party!

(*Mac starts singing, then some of the girls join in. Meanwhile more and more people come on from Cannery Row,
as if they had heard a message by native wireless, and the
number grows into a song and dance.*)

MAC:
   Party comin' up on Cannery Row,
CROWD:
   Party comin' up on Cannery Row.
GIRLS:
   Hear the rumble over Cannery Row?
CROWD:
   Hear the rumble over Cannery Row?
MAC:
   Rumblin', mumblin', murmurin' low.
CROWD:
   Rumblin', mumblin', murmurin' low.
MAC:
      Like a cyclone, ready to blow!
CROWD:
      Like a cyclone, ready to blow!
ALL:
   Gettin' ready to pop,
   Gettin' ready to bust,
   Gettin' ready to blow!

A NEWCOMER:
    When do we go?
CROWD:
    Tomorrer.
NEWCOMER:
    Tomorrer?
ALL:
    Tomorrer! Tomorrer! Tomorrer!

act two: scene 2

Cannery Row.

MAC:

Oh there never was a party
   like the party that we're going to have tomorrow
      night!
What a sweetheart of a party!
   We'll be rowdy, loud and hearty till the sun gets
      bright!
Oh there never was a clambake we recall
Or a rumpus or a ruckus or a ball
Like the party that we're going to have tomorrow night,
The best damn party of all!

ALL:

Oh there never was a party
   like the party that we're going to have tomorrow
      night!

HAZEL:

What a sweetheart of a party!
   We'll be drinking a la carty till the stars turn white.

AGNES:

Oh, the crowd has never had itself a ball
Like that history-making, record-breaking brawl,

ALL:

Like that party that we're going to have tomorrow night,
The best damn party of all!

(*A dance follows exit of crowd.*)

act two: scene 3

The Palace Flophouse, the following night.

This is the reverse angle of the Act One version of the Flophouse. A door right, facing the audience, leads into the interior, so that the exterior effect is downstage. The Flophouse has been decorated for the occasion, of course. There is a bower of pine boughs crossed to make a canopy. The great stove is laid out as a bar and the oven is full of cracked ice. Across the back and in front of the back wall is a little stage now concealed by a painter's drop cloth used as a curtain. Japanese lanterns are decked across the front of the house. As the curtain rises, Mac and some of the boys are busy finishing these decorations. Over in the corner down left Eddie is giving careful lessons to Johnny Carriagra in the art of palming cards. Johnny is not dressed as Cupid yet, but he has the props over his T-shirt at this point, bow, arrow, and quiver.

EDDIE: Now try it again, Johnny.
  (*Johnny tries to palm the card.*)

No! I can see the edge of it. Look. Sort of squeeze the edges in your palm, like this. Now try it again.
(*Mac stands back and surveys the decorations.*)

MAC: A veritable fairyland!
(*The other boys nod reverently, admiring as usual Mac's talent for turning a phrase.*)

EDDIE (*to Johnny*): That's good. Now let's see you get it out of the jar. You make a pass with the bow, like this, so they'll look at your other hand, and you say—

JOHNNY: I know. (*He recites*) I am Cupid, God of love, and I draw a bead on unsuspecting hearts.

GEORGE: God, that's beautiful. Where'd you get that, Mac?

MAC: I made it up.

EDDIE (*to Johnny*): Now, when you shove up the bow with your right hand, you get the ticket out of the jar with your left. Try it.
(*One of the Flophouse gang enters with a tin tray. He sees the bottle on the table and makes a grab for it. He drops the tray with a clatter.*)

MAC: Why don't you watch what you're doing!
(*The character goes to reassure Mac unsteadily, and his hand squashes down on a cake on the table. Mac and George groan, "There goes the cake," etc. As the character raises his hand we see that it is covered with white icing. He exits.*)

GEORGE: Crowd ought to be here soon.

MAC: They won't come till they get the signal—
(*A scream is heard offstage, in the direction where the*

"cake spoiler" has gone. A girl enters with a small vase of seedy-looking flowers which she places on the table. As she turns her back to the audience to exit, we see the very definite imprint of a hand—in white icing! There are obvious reactions from the boys and Mac holds his hand over Johnny's eyes when he starts to stare at the girl.)

EDDIE (*after girl's exit*): Now try it again, Johnny.

JOHNNY (*brandishing the bow*): I am Cupid, God of love. I draw a bead on unsuspecting hearts.

EDDIE: That's good, but don't look at your left hand, Johnny. Take the jar. And dig around the cards without dropping the ticket. Go on, practice.

GEORGE: Say, Mac, where's Hazel?

MAC: He wanted to come as Prince Charming. One of the dames is fixin' his costume.

(*Doc enters, dressed for the tide pool as he was in Act One, Scene 1, carrying a pail. He opens the door, and without coming into the Flophouse talks through the door at Mac.*)

DOC: Hey, Mac, I dropped in to tell you I can't come tonight.

MAC: Aw, Doc, you *gotta* come! What's the matter?

DOC: Goin' down to the tide pool. Don't feel like playin' tonight. Feel like working.

GEORGE: But Doc, you gotta stay for the raffle!

MAC: No matter what, you gotta stay for the rafflle!

DOC: I'd only be a wet blanket.

(*He starts to go. Mac comes through the door and grabs his arm.*)

MAC: Look, Doc! The crowd is comin'! Stay a coupla minutes. I'll run the raffle off right away, honest! Please, Doc! For me!

(*A trumpet call is heard offstage. Mac and George hastily clear the ladder which they have been using to finish the decorations. The crowd starts to enter and cross the stage toward the door. It is led by Pancho playing the trumpet dressed in a weird outfit. The music of "The Party That We're Going to Have" is played. As the crowd crosses we see its members have dressed themselves in various costumes: "Happys," "Sneezeys," "Dopeys," "Grumpys," etc. Ray arrives in a wheelbarrow; he represents "Sleepy." The barrow is being pushed by Joe who for some odd reason is dressed as Dracula. There is a "Miss Flophouse," and Eddie arrives as an overstuffed chair, followed by a wild Conga line representing a mad assortment of imaginary characters. Doc, who has tried to leave, is caught up by the parade and taken into the party, since they give him no time to protest. Finally Hazel arrives and creates quite a sensation. The basis of his costume is long gray underwear, to which have been sewed hearts, diamonds, spades, and clubs in red and black. A silver-painted football helmet on his head carries a huge feather plume. Pompons adorn his shoes. There is a large paper ruff around his neck, and from the belt around his middle hangs a scabbard holding a large wooden sword. He brings with him on a long rein a horse composed of a broomhandle for a neck and a painted bucket for a head. The body of the horse con-*)

sists of Alec in front and Whitey behind, both covered with an old blanket. Below the horse's head we see that Alec is as usual smoking a cigar. Nothing can be seen of Whitey, but the rear end of the horse staggers perceptibly. Hazel lifts his sword proudly as he speaks.)

HAZEL: I am Prince Charming. I proteck damsels.

(*There is scattered and puzzled applause. Mac comes forward sympathetically and puts a hand on Hazel's shoulder. Pancho jumps up on the table and, prompted by Mac, starts to play some wild music, at which point a wild dance starts, ending with a bedlam of noise. Mac gets up on the table and shouts at the crowd.*)

MAC: Quiet! Quiet, everybody!

(*They quiet down.*)

We got certain ceremonies to perform here this evenin', and I'm goin' to start them now before you all get so damn plastered you don't know what's goin' on. (*He walks over to Doc and puts his hand on his shoulder.*) Fellow citizens, right here in Cannery Row lives a guy that there can't nobody want a better friend. For years we have took his bounty without sharing nothing back at him. Now this guy needs a certain article that runs into dough. Therefore it is the pleasure of I and the boys to raffle off the Palace Flophouse, so we can buy a microscope for Doc! We got three hundred and eighty bucks. Curtain!

(*Applause.*)

DOC: Mac, you're crazy!

MAC: Wait a minute. (*Going up to the curtain*) Are we all ready? Are you all right back there, Johnny?

JOHNNY (*from behind curtain*): I'm damn cold back here!

MAC: Curtain!

(*The cloth is pulled aside to reveal Johnny dressed in an aluminum supporter and a pair of blue paper wings.*)

JOHNNY (*brandishing his bow*): I am Cupid, God of love.

(*The winning ticket slips from his palm and flutters to the floor. Johnny scrambles after it, yelling*) I draw a bead on unexpected hearts. (*He grabs the ticket and turns to Mac*) What do I do now?

MAC: Oh, what the hell! . . . Is that the ticket you have drawn, Cupid?

JOHNNY: I have plucked from the many.

MAC: Give it to me, you little—(*He turns to the crowd.*) Friends, do my eyes deceive me? This *is* a surprise! Well, well! Folks, it gives me great pleasure to announce that the Palace Flophouse has passed into the hands of Doc!

(*A roar of laughter goes up and several people crowd around Doc to congratulate him, and the whole party starts to get very disorderly indeed. The first fight is even starting as Mac pulls the assailants apart, holds up his hand, and shouts*)

What are you trying to do, louse up the party? The *pageant* is about to begin.

(*Music is heard. Fauna enters dressed as the head witch. She walks majestically downstage.*)

MAC: This here from Snow White and the Seven Dwarfs is the head witch.

FAUNA (*singing*):

Come out, all ye witches,
Come out, all ye witches!

(*She looks up at the curtain. Nothing happens and she shouts irritably*) Come out, you witches!

(*Four of her girls come out, all dressed as witches.*)

GIRLS (*singing*):

We are a gang of witches,
We are a witch's mob.
We got it in for Snow White,
She's nothin' but a slob—

HAZEL (*patting Mac on the back*): How do you do it, Mac?

MAC: Genius.

GIRLS:

We'll put her on a broomstick
And take her for a ride.
We'll drop her in a lime pit—
She'll be no prince's bride!

HAZEL: I am Prince Charming. I proteck damsels.

MAC: Go back, Hazel! Some other time!

FAUNA (*to Mac*): Where was we?

MAC (*sotto voce*): This is where it turns out you ain't no witch at all.

(*Two girls come from either side and pull off Fauna's black witch's robe. Fauna removes her witch's hat. Applause from the crowd. Johnny comes from the side and hands her a wand, which is a toilet brush dressed up with silver paper.*)

FAUNA (*reciting*): I ain't no witch at all! I am Snow White's fairy godmother.

(*All the other witches cringe. She waves her wand.*)

Now I make all of you fairy godmothers!

(*The girls drop their black dominos and emerge as beautiful fairy godmothers. Everybody applauds, as they applauded Fauna's transformation. The girls now make a V-shaped path up to the center of the curtain, hold out their hands high, and start to build up Snow White's entrance.*)

GIRLS (*singing*):

Welcome to Snow White,

All hail Snow White!

ALL:

Snow White, Snow White, Snow White, Snow White.

(*There is a pause. The curtains do not part.*)

FAUNA (*shouting*): Come on the hell out of there, Snow White.

(*The curtains part and Suzy enters.*)

GIRLS (*in unison*): Snow White!

FAUNA: Now I give all of you Snow White, the bride!

(*She looks over at Doc. The orchestra strikes a chord. Suzy steps forward.*)

FAUNA (*looking over at Doc to see what effect Suzy has made*): Snow White will now sing "Will You Marry Me?" from the Hit Parade!

(Suzy steps forward and sings with quiet and shy sincerity, never once daring to look at Doc)

SUZY:

    Will you marry me?
    All I own I want you to share.
    This is not to be
    Any light, summer-night love affair.
    Like a ship at sea,
    Vainly I looked for a shore.
    Say you'll marry me?
    And I will look no more!

(Now Fauna gets behind Suzy, puts her arm around her and marches up and down, "sister act" fashion. As they sing the refrain together, Fauna keeps trying to point Suzy straight at Doc. He becomes conscious that Fauna is being very obvious in having Suzy sing in his direction, virtually proposing to him.)

FAUNA AND SUZY:

    Will you marry me?
    All I own I want you to share.

This is not to be
Any light, summer-night love affair.

(Several of the guests start to cry, because this is the stage of the evening when alcohol has a very sentimental and softening effect on some.)

GIRL: It's so beautiful.

ALL (*joining in*):
Like a ship at sea,
Vainly I looked for a shore.
Say you'll marry me?
And I will look no more!

FAUNA: Doc, your bride!

DOC: What the hell is going on?

SUZY (*deeply humiliated*): Nothin'! It's a gag of Fauna's. I was makin' like Snow White—

FAUNA: And you was the Prince—get it!

DOC (*getting it*): Oh, well—why didn't somebody tell me? (*With an elaborate gesture*) Fairy Godmother, I accept my bride.

SUZY (*on the point of tears*): I heard you the first time. (*She turns away, looking at the floor.*)

DOC (*singing*):
Will you marry me?
All I own I want you to share—

SUZY (*taking off her veil*): We had enough of this damn foolishness.

DOC:
   This is not to be
   Any light, summer-night love affair . . .
SUZY: You accept your bride! Who the hell would want you?
   (*She runs outside. Fauna follows.*)
FAUNA: Why'd you talk that way to Doc?
SUZY: He don't think I'm good enough for him. I see it in his
   eyes. He don't think I'm good enough—and I don't think
   so either!
   (*She dashes off. Doc comes through the door.*)
FAUNA: Where you goin'?
DOC: Home!
FAUNA: Oh!
   (*He exits in the direction opposite to that which Suzy
   took. From here on the scene builds up to bedlam, a bed-
   lam of many counterpoints. The band keeps playing, and
   most of the guests keep dancing. Sometimes they bump
   into one another and start to fight.*)
MAC (*coming out of door, to Fauna, real tears in his voice*):
   Every party we give winds up in a rhubarb! A rhubarb!
   (*Fauna opens her arms to him and he weeps on her
   motherly bosom.*)

act two: scene 4

Cannery Row, next day.

Jim is pacing up and down thoughtfully.

JIM (*as Marjorie enters*): Good morning, Marjorie.
MARJORIE: 'Mornin', Jim.
JIM: How was the party last night?
  (*Marjorie gestures to him that she can't even talk about it, and continues off down street. George enters, pushing Ray in wheelbarrow.*)
  Hi, George—where are you goin'?
GEORGE: I'm takin' my brother-in-law back to his home. And I don't think he's going to take his wife her breakfast on a tray this morning.
  (*As George exits, Suzy enters and goes directly to Jim.*)
SUZY: Jim!
JIM: Hello, Suzy.
SUZY: I want to talk to you. (*Getting down to business*) You remember once you said if I wanted to blow town you'd lend me the dough?
JIM: Sure I remember, but—

SUZY: I wonder could you stake me *not* to blow town?

JIM: What's up?

SUZY: I got a job. Waitress over at Christine's hamburger joint.

JIM: Can Christine afford to give you a salary?

SUZY: No—but she'll feed me over there.

JIM: Where you goin' to live?

SUZY (*turning and pointing*): I thought I'd try that pipe down there.

JIM: The boiler?

SUZY: Yeh. Other people have lived there before.

JIM: That's right. Why do you call it a pipe?

SUZY: It sounds cooler than when you call it a boiler.

JIM: One thing about it, you don't have to pay rent there.

SUZY: That's what I figured. Will you help me?

JIM (*putting his hand in his pocket*): I staked kids before. What the hell have I got to lose?

SUZY: Twenty-five dollars—but you'll get it back.

JIM (*handing it to her*): I know I will.

SUZY: Thanks.

> (*Suzy exits. Jim looks after and hums or sings a few lines of "All Kinds of People," during which interlude Hazel comes on looking dejected, even harried. He groans.*)

JIM: Hi, Hazel. What *really* happened at that party over at the Flophouse?

HAZEL: It gets me mixed up when I even try to think of it. I was there, and I can't tell you what happened. All I know is nothin' seems any good any more.

JIM : Why do you say that?

HAZEL : Doc ain't himself, and if Doc ain't himself, who the
hell am I? Know what I mean?

JIM (*smiling*): I thought Mac had some ideas about helping
Doc.

HAZEL : Mac goofed. That mixes me up more when I think
of that. In fact, Jim, it's hard for me to think of anything. Is
it hard for you to think, Jim?

JIM : Sure. It's hard for everybody.

HAZEL : It's harder for me.

(*He sings*)

I suffer somethin' awful when I think.
Thinkin' puts my brain on the blink.
I feel a kind of a tickin'
And a scrapin' in my head
Like a million skaters clickin' round a rink!
And here's the part that always gets me sore—
Thinkin' never changes the score.
By the time you make yer mind up
It's a cinch you're gonna wind up

Behind the eight ball like you was before!

(*Music is played under the following dialogue.*)

When I got somethin' important to think about, I go and hide under a tree so I can be alone and nobody can bother me. Then I add it all up, dope it out—kinda mule it over. Hardest thing for me is to remember what the problem *is*. It goes away from me and I chase it and then other things come in between it and me, like they was tryin' to trip me up . . .
(*He sings again*)
I grit my teeth
An' shut my eyes
An' I screw my eyebrows together
An' I cover my ears so there ain't no chance to hear.
(*He puts his hands on his ears and speaks*)
Like this.
(*He sings again*)
I stay this way fer a minute er two
An' try to think a problem through,
To dig and dig and dig fer a big ideer!
Then I open my eyes
An' ungrit my teeth
An' I separate my eyebrows
An' I take my hand off my ear so I can hear.
I pull my thoughts together
An' I tie them in a knot.
Then I look at what I got—

(*The music swells to a very loud triumphant chord, and
Hazel speaks the next word*)

Nothin'!

(*Music continues.*)

JIM: Do you have to do that with every problem, Hazel?

HAZEL: Oh no! Gee, no! Lotta problems come up are very
simple for me, things I can handle without thinkin' about.
Say I'm havin' a argument with a feller and he says somethin' I don't like. *I* say, "Whatsa matter with you? You
stupid or somethin'?" I tell him, "Drop dead . . . turn
blue!" I know how to handle myself like that all right. But
when somethin' comes up that never come up before and I
start askin' myself questions I don't know the answer to
them—man, that's rugged!

(*He sings*)

A feller gets in trouble when he thinks,

Thinkin' gets your brain full o' kinks!

Once you let a problem face you

And you try to face it back,

It'll foller you an' chase you like a jinx.

I'm better off to let a problem be—

Half 'a time it blows out to sea.

That's the only way to trick it,

See? If I don't try to lick it

It ain't got any chance o' lickin' me!

(*Music continues.*)

JIM: So why are you beating your brains out now?

HAZEL: This is for Doc! He needs my help. Ain't that funny,

a guy who can think as good as he can? I gotta help *him*. I bet thinkin' got him into all this trouble.

JIM: Maybe you're right, Hazel. Maybe there's altogether too much thinkin' going on.

HAZEL: It's unhealthy. Just the same, Doc's in this and I gotta get him out of it . . . Jim, would you mind very much if I asked you to leave me? I just gotta be alone so I can find a way to get Doc out o' trouble.

JIM: Sure.

(*He smiles and leaves. Now Hazel goes into the kind of trance he described earlier. We have the rare experience of watching Hazel's mind work. Naturally he has to sing a little slower this time while he reasons.*)

HAZEL:

It all begun
When he meets a broad
An' he says he's writin' a paper
Which is gonna be full o' that scientific crap—
Then right away it's a federal case!
He won't let no one in his place,
An' Mac says Doc's been caught in a cul-de-sap!
Then the fourth o' July
Come along last night
An' it falls right on Doc's birthday.
When he sings "Will You Marry Me?" Suzy runs away—
Could Suzy be the reason
Why Doc is in a rut,
An' goin' off his nut? . . .

(The orchestra rises to great heights and brilliant chords which describe the complicated process of Hazel's thinking and the torture of it all. Then the music stops. A vacant expression comes into Hazel's now open eyes. He speaks.)
What was the problem?
(He walks off the stage with clenched fists and closed eyes, deep in thought again, trying to get it back as the lights fade out quickly.)

act two: scene 5

Outside the Bear Flag Cafe, a few weeks later.

The inside of the room is barely visible. Fauna sits at the window looking out onto Cannery Row. Joe enters from the right. His hair is combed stiff and shiny. He wears a flower in his lapel. He is in a gay and adventurous mood. Esteban, the tenor from Sonny Boy's, trails after him.

J O E : Hiya, Fauna?

F A U N A : Hello, Joe.

J O E *(to Esteban)*: Espera me poi alli.
    (Esteban nods and exits. Then Joe speaks to Fauna, pointing up to the sky.)
    Beautiful moon.

F A U N A *(squinting at him, trying to size up the situation)*: Yeh.

J O E : No night for a young girl to stay shut up in a boiler.

F A U N A : You talkin' about Suzy?

J O E : Up to a couple of weeks ago I would have said she was just one more tramp. Then she broke loose and moved into that pipe there, and I begin to think she's got more to her than I figured.

FAUNA: She's on a kick where she wants to do everything all by herself. I offered to give her some furniture. She wouldn't have any of it. I told her she could come over here and take a bath whenever she wanted to. No. They got a shower down where she works.

JOE: How do you get into that pipe?

FAUNA: Ain't no way except through the fire door and that's too small for me to crawl into.

JOE (*looking off and smiling*): Me—I think I can make it. (*He starts to go.*)

FAUNA: She's Doc's!

JOE: Dames don't belong to nobody.
(*Joe exits.*)

FAUNA (*calling after him*): I got an idea this one does—no matter what she says and no matter what he says.
(*As if she hears Doc's footsteps coming down the street she turns her head as Doc enters.*)

DOC: How are you, Fauna!

FAUNA: Hello, Doc. I was just—(*looking off down the street in the direction of the Mexican*) thinkin' about you.

DOC: That's a coincidence. I was just thinking about myself.

FAUNA: Got problems?

DOC: Sort of.
(*Offstage, Esteban starts singing "All at Once," in Spanish. Doc looks off.*)
Who's that?

FAUNA: Joe and the wetback from Sonny Boy's serenading Suzy, I think.

DOC: You're kidding!

FAUNA: No, I ain't.

DOC: Okay, let him.

FAUNA: Sure. It ain't anybody's business except his and Suzy's.

DOC: Certainly no business of mine.

FAUNA: Don't try to kid Grandma.

DOC: Fauna, this girl and I would murder each other. She's one of those kids who doesn't know anything but she's sure about everything. You know what'll happen to her after she's been married for about two months to some poor guy? She'll become a prude.

FAUNA: A prude?

DOC: Yes, a prude. I know. There is no possible way for this girl and me to get together. Is that clear?

FAUNA: It's clear that you been thinkin' about it a lot.

DOC: Maybe I have! But thank God I've got sense enough to keep me from doing anything crazy . . .
(*The singing offstage stops and Doc looks off.*)
What's he trying to do?

FAUNA: Trying to get in that fire door.
(*There is the sound of the clank of an iron door offstage.*)

DOC (*happily*): She slammed it on him!

FAUNA: So she did!

DOC: Good for her!
(*Esteban starts to sing again.*)

FAUNA: Joe ain't put off easy. He's got the right idea about girls. You keep after 'em long enough, chances are you'll get 'em.

DOC: Thanks for the coaching, Fauna, but it won't do any good. I don't want her. I don't want her and what's more I know I can't have her. (*He looks off again.*)

FAUNA (*quietly*): You can't *not* have her either, Doc. Whatever happens, you've got her.

DOC: You're nuts! (*He looks off and starts to mutter under his breath.*) What the hell does he think he's doing, the son of a—

(*He runs off, a fierce expression on his face that bodes no good for Joe. Fauna smiles and starts to sing, a happy philosopher.*)

FAUNA:

The romance that you have waited for
Will come when it comes.
Without a word of warning it will start.
With a sudden blare of trumpets and the rattle of drums
A dream will take possession of your heart . . .

You start to light
Her cigarette,
And all at once
You love her.
You've scarcely talked,
You've scarcely met,
And all at once
You love her.

You like her eyes,
You tell her so.
She thinks you're wise
And clever.
You kiss good night,
And then you know
You'll kiss good night
Forever!
You wonder where
Your heart can go—
Then all at once you know.

(The lights fade.)

act two: scene 6

Cannery Row, next evening.

Cannery Row is gloomy. Silent groups pace past one another. George enters. The others look at him questioningly, as if asking, "Any news?" He shakes his head.

MABEL: Why is he walkin' up and down?
HAZEL: He's been walkin' up and down like that for an hour!
MAC: Outside Suzy's boiler!
   (*Fauna enters.*)
AGNES: Hey, Fauna, know anything about Doc?
FAUNA: Sure. I know he almost murdered the Mexican for trying to get in that pipe.
MAC: Look out, here he comes!
   (*Doc enters, carrying flowers. He stops suddenly and faces them. His attitude and speech border on violence.*)
DOC: What are you looking at? . . . I'll tell you! You're looking at a man who's scared stiff—scared of a girl who lives in a boiler—(*He throws the flowers on the ground.*) Scared that if he knocks on that door she won't let him in.

FAUNA: One thing sure. You won't get in if you *don't* knock!

HAZEL: Whyn't you go up and say: "Come on the hell out of that boiler and fight!"

DOC: Thanks, Hazel.

FAUNA: That ain't bad advice, Doc.

(*She puts her hand on Doc's shoulder and starts to sing*)

Stand up to the girl like a man.

GIRLS:

Stand up to the girl like a man!

FAUNA:

Just let her know you run the show
And she'll go along with the plan.

BOYS:

Stand up to the girl like a guy
Stand up to the girl like a guy.

HAZEL:

And tell her to behave herself
Or you'll put a mouse on her eye.

FAUNA:

If she wants to make you wait,
Don't get in no big debate.

Don't beg and plead and pray to the girl—
But stand right up and say to the girl—
ALL:
How long

And say to the girl,
And say to the girl:
FAUNA:

How long
Do we gotta talk it over?
How long
Do we gotta horse around?
I tell you to yer face I want you and you drive me nuts,
But all I ever get from you is ifs and ands and buts!
How long
Do we gotta race the motor
Before we can really get to go?
How long
Do you make a feller guess how sweet you are,
Before you will really let him know?

(*Now Doc's male friends try to exhort him.*)

BOYS:
The man you used to be
Would make a fricassee
Of any chick who tried to get tough!
DOC (*beginning to feel stronger*):
The man I used to be
Had an old recipe

For calling any feminine bluff—
You start in sweet and gentle,
Then you wind up firm and rough!

FAUNA AND GIRLS:

That's the stuff!

BOYS:

Stand up to the girl!

ALL:

Stand up to the girl!

DOC:

I'll say to the girl—

ALL:

You'll say to the girl:

DOC:

How long—
(*He looks for prompting.*)

ALL:

Do we gotta talk it over!

DOC:

How long
Do we gotta horse around!
How long do you believe that you can keep me on the
    hook?
How long do you believe that you can play me for a
    schnook?
How long
Must I walk alone at evening
While stars squander silver on the sea?

How long
Till you open up your arms and let me know
How warm and how lovely they can be?

MAC:

Toughen it up!

ALL:

Toughen up!

GIRLS:

Stand up to the girl like a man—

MEN:

Stand up to the girl like a man—

GIRLS:

Stand up to the girl like a man—

MEN:

Stand up to the girl like a man—

ALL:

Good luck to you, Doc. You'll need it!
Good luck to you, Doc. You'll need it!
Good luck to you, Doc.
Good luck to you, Doc. You'll need it when you say to her:
How long? How long? How long?

*(They now sing a special choral arrangement of the re-
frain, during which a girl picks up Doc's flowers and hands
them to Fauna. Fauna puts the flowers into Doc's hands,
smoothes his hair, pats his lapel, and sends him off to vic-
tory!)*

act two: scene 7

Inside "The Pipe."

It has been fixed up cosily by Suzy, within the architectural limitations of a boiler's interior.

Suzy is discovered sitting on a cot doing some embroidery. There is a knock on the door. Suzy takes a deep breath, gets up, takes a passing look and a primp in the mirror. There is another rap on the door, even louder.

SUZY (*opening the fire door*): Hey, do you want to break down the door?

DOC (*appearing in the opening*): I was just about to. (*He is still infused with the determination given him by his pals.*) Take these flowers! I'm coming in!

SUZY (*taking them, and not quite knowing how to handle the situation*): Thanks. Don't stand up.

DOC (*indignantly*): Why shouldn't I stand up?

SUZY: Because you'll hit your head.

DOC (*repulsed for the first time*): Oh . . . look here, Suzy, I came to talk to you.

SUZY: Okay, sit down.

(*Doc sits down automatically.*)

I'm makin' a cup of tea on the Sterno. Want some?

DOC: Yes, I guess so. Thanks. (*Determination coming back to him*) Suzy, how long—

SUZY: Won't be a minute. The tea's already made. (*She pours the tea.*) I'm makin' good tips at the hamburger joint. I paid off Jim Blaikey in two weeks.

DOC (*almost angrily*): You sound happy.

SUZY: I am. You know who did it for me?

DOC: No, who?

SUZY: Fauna. She made me proud, and I ain't never been proud before in my life. She said there ain't anything in the world like Suzy.

DOC: Fauna tried to do a job on me, too, but I don't think it's working so well. I guess I'd better make up my own words.

SUZY: So what do you want to say?

DOC: Suzy, I'm sorry for what happened.

SUZY: It wasn't any fault of yours, but it sure as hell give me a lesson. I had myself a good cry and now it's done. I don't want to talk about it any more.

DOC: I would do anything to—

SUZY: Look, Doc. There's nothing for you to do. I don't need anything. Anybody's sorry for me, they're wastin' their time. Whatever's got to be done I'm doin' it all myself! If you can get that through your knocker, okay. If you can't, take a powder.

DOC: I think I can get it through my knocker.

(*They each take a sip of tea.*)

Suzy, could you tell me—what you want in a man?

SUZY (*putting her cup and saucer on box*): If I thought it wasn't a pitch you were making, I'd tell you.

DOC (*putting his cup and saucer on box*): I don't think it's a pitch.

SUZY: Okay then. Maybe what I want ain't anywhere in the world, but I want it, so I think there is such a thing. I want a guy that's wide open. He can be tough, but I want a window in him. He can have his guard up every other place, but not with me. And he's got to need the hell out of me. He's got to be the kind of guy that if he ain't got me he ain't got nothin'!

DOC: I hope you'll find him, Suzy.

SUZY: If I do, one thing I know—I'm goin' to play it careful. I'm not goin' to blow another chance. I may be dumb, but I ain't as dumb as I was.

(*She sings*)
I leapt before I looked
        And I got hooked.
I played with fire and burned—
        That's how I learned.
I must admit I owe a lot to you.
From now on I will know what not to do.

The next time it happens
I'll be wise enough to know
Not to trust my eyesight when my eyes begin to glow.
The next time I'm in love
With anyone like you,
My heart will sing no love song till I know the words are
        true.
"The next time it happens"—
What a foolish thing to say!
Who expects a miracle to happen every day?
It isn't in the cards
As far as I can see
That a thing so beautiful and wonderful
Could happen more than once to me.

(The music of the verse is taken up after the refrain. Doc takes a step toward Suzy. She turns away.)

Please don't say anything.

DOC: I wasn't going to.

SUZY: Talkin' about it is a waste of time.

DOC: I know. One thing about a balloon. Once you bust it, it's bust for good.

SUZY: Bingo!

DOC (*quietly*): You're not the only one who learned something from this. We're even.

(He sings)

The next time it happens
I'll be wise enough to know
Not to trust my eyesight when my eyes begin to glow.
The next time I'm in love
With anyone like you,
My heart will sing no love song till I know the words are
  true.
"The next time it happens"—
What a foolish thing to say!
Who expects a miracle to happen every day?
It isn't in the cards
As far as I can see
That a thing so beautiful and wonderful
Could happen more than once to me.

(He goes towards the door, stops and calls back to Suzy, over his shoulder.)

Good-by.

SUZY: Good-by.

(*Doc stoops down at the fire door, then rises again.*)

DOC: I feel sorta silly crawling through that door with you watching me.

SUZY: I'll turn around.

(*She is glad to turn around so he won't see her tears. Doc crawls out. She sings*)

It isn't in the cards

As far as I can see

That a thing so beautiful and wonderful

Could happen more than once to me.

(*She throws herself on the cot and buries her head in the pillow. Presently there is a knock on the fire door. She looks up. She looks in the mirror again—apparently she thinks it's Doc coming back. She runs to the door, hesitates, and then opens it. There are two different legs there, and the man stoops over and shows his face. It is Hazel.*)

HAZEL: What'd you do to Doc?

SUZY: I didn't do anything to him.

HAZEL: When he left here I passed him and he hardly said hello to me.

SUZY (*turning away*): I didn't tell him not to say hello to you.

HAZEL: Doc's in some kind of trouble. Anybody in trouble, why, they go to him. He helps everybody. Once he went character witness for me, and I ain't got no character. . . . Can't you help him somehow?

SUZY: What could *I* do?

HAZEL: Well, couldn't you go over and set with him?

SUZY: No. Why should I go over and set with him?

HAZEL: Don't you like him?

SUZY: I like him all right.

HAZEL: Well, why don't you do somethin' for him?

SUZY: I don't even know what's wrong with him. If he was in any real trouble, you know, like if he was sick or if he bust his leg or an arm or something—

HAZEL: What would you do then?

SUZY: Oh, I don't know. I'd probably go over and take him some soup or something.

HAZEL: If he bust an arm or a leg, huh?

(*He looks dangerously thoughtful as the lights fade.*)

act two: scene 8

Cannery Row, a few hours later.

*Hazel enters and walks slowly, deep in thought. The music of
"Thinkin'" is played underneath the action. It now rises to
loud and discordant and painful heights. Hazel carries a baseball
bat. Mac enters, waves to Hazel. Mac suddenly realizes that
Hazel was carrying a baseball bat, and he looks off, scratching
his head in puzzlement.*

act two: scene 9

The Western Biological Laboratory, next morning.

Dr. Horace Dormody is just finishing putting a splint on Doc's arm.

DORMODY: This'll hold it together all right. It's a clean break —take some time to heal.

DOC: It's the damn'dest most mysterious thing I ever heard of. I wake up and I've got a broken arm!
(*The doctor goes about closing his bag.*)
What do you make of it, Doc?

DORMODY: Looks to me like somebody hit it with a club.

DOC: But that's impossible. There was nobody in here. Only thing I can figure is I must have turned over and caught my arm between the wall and the bed.

DORMODY (*drily*): Try not to bump into things. I'll come in to see you tomorrow. So long.

DOC: I won't be here. I've got to go down to La Jolla. The spring tides start tomorrow.

DORMODY: How are you going to turn over those heavy
   rocks?

DOC: I've got to.

DORMODY: Good luck.
   (*He goes out the door. Just as he emerges from Doc's
   house, Suzy enters, and immediately anxiety crosses her
   face.*)
   Good morning, Suzy.
   (*Meanwhile Doc goes up to the kitchen alcove and starts
   rummaging in the sectional bookcases for a can of soup.*)

SUZY (*as she meets the doctor*): I just saw you coming out of
   Doc's place. Anything the matter?

DORMODY: Doc broke his arm.

SUZY: How?

DORMODY: He says he got it caught between the bed and the
   wall—in his sleep.

SUZY: How can you break an arm that way?

DORMODY: You can't.
   (*He goes on down the street. Suzy walks to Doc's door,
   hesitates, turns away, then turns back again, and knocks.*)

DOC: Come in!
   (*Suzy puts her hand on the knob and hesitates again. Doc
   calls louder*)
   Come in!
   (*Suzy opens the door. They stand there looking at each
   other in silence. Suzy goes into Doc's house and closes the
   door softly. Hazel runs on suddenly and listens at the door.*)

SUZY: Doctor Dormody says you broke your arm.

DOC: I did, but God knows how.

SUZY (*indicating the can of soup in his hand*): What are you doing with that?

DOC: I was just figuring I'd make myself some soup.

SUZY: With one hand? Give me that. Sit down and rest.

(*Doc obeys. Suzy takes the can. During the following scene she is sometimes on stage and sometimes off, in connection with preparing the soup. Hazel, listening at the door, is delirious with happiness. Mac enters and catches him with his eye at the keyhole.*)

MAC: Hazel, what the hell are you doin'? Spyin' on Doc?

(*Hazel stands up.*)

What's *he* doin'?

HAZEL: He's just sittin'.

MAC: I got the boys comin' over with the microscope. We're goin' to make the presentation.

HAZEL: You can't go in now.

MAC: Why not?

HAZEL: Doc broke his arm.

MAC: How?

HAZEL: It ain't important how. The main thing is he's got Suzy in there makin' soup for him, see?

MAC: No!

HAZEL: Take a look.

(*Mac looks in the keyhole. Doc calls to Suzy. He has picked up a letter that is on the table next to his chair.*)

DOC: Suzy!

SUZY (*entering from kitchen with pan*): Yeh?

DOC: When I got home last night there was a letter waiting for me from Cal. Tech.

SUZY: What's that?

DOC: California Institute of Technology.

(*Pause.*)

SUZY: What do you know?

(*The orchestra begins the refrain of "The Next Time It Happens."*)

DOC: I could teach and do research there. Think I ought to?

SUZY: Why not, if you want to?

DOC: I don't like to work for anybody.

SUZY: Then tell 'em to go to hell. (*She continues at her work.*)

DOC: On the other hand, they'd let me read my paper before the Academy of Science.

SUZY: Do it, then.

DOC: And they've got a lot of wonderful equipment there.

SUZY: Fine.

DOC: I don't even know whether I can write the damn paper. What shall I do, Suzy?

SUZY: What do you want to do?

DOC: I don't know.

SUZY: What's wrong with that? Just don't do anything.

HAZEL (*nudging Mac*): She said if he bust his arm she'd take some soup over to him, and there she is in there cookin' the soup.

MAC: If he bust his arm—who did she say that to?

HAZEL: Me.

(*Now he stoops down and peeks through the keyhole. Mac does some deep thinking. Agnes passes.*)

AGNES: What's Hazel looking at?

MAC (*in a hoarse whisper*): Suzy's in there with Doc.

(*Agnes doesn't wait a second but runs off the stage.*)

DOC: I don't know what I'm going to do about the spring tides at La Jolla. I've got to go tonight.

SUZY: How you going to drive a car with one hand?

DOC: I can't. Do you drive?

SUZY: Sure. That is, I could if you sat beside me and told me what to do.

DOC (*smiling*): It doesn't sound very safe. Anyway, there are rocks down there that weigh fifty or a hundred pounds. Pretty hard to turn over.

SUZY: I ain't put together with spit.

(*Doc smiles at Suzy. A silent pause, then Suzy turns suddenly and goes back to the kitchen. Outside the door Mac pulls Hazel away from the keyhole.*)

MAC: Refresh my memory. What was you doin' with that baseball bat last night?

(*Hazel quickly puts his face back to the keyhole.*)

Oh no!

SUZY: The soup is on the fire. You can pour it into the plate with your left hand, I guess.

DOC: Where are you going?

SUZY: To work. (*She starts for the door.*)

DOC: I thought you were going to La Jolla with me.

SUZY: You didn't say so.

DOC: Suzy—
> (*She stops very near the door and waits for him to go on.*)
> Suzy, *will* you come to La Jolla with me?
> (*She hesitates. She thinks. She does not turn.*)
> Suzy, I love you. I need the hell out of you.
> (*Suzy whirls around and faces Doc. Then she takes a slow breath and her eyes shine with incredible excitement.*)

SUZY: . . . Brother, you got yourself a girl!
> (*She moves slowly to him. He rises from his chair. They kiss. Mac pulls Hazel up on his feet.*)

MAC: You know, Hazel, I think you'd have made a hell of a President at that.
> (*Fauna comes running on as fast as she can, with a few of the girls behind her.*)

FAUNA: Where are they?

HAZEL: In there.

FAUNA: What are they doin'?

MAC: He's kissin' her.
> (*Fauna throws Mac and Hazel out of the way and leans over to look through the keyhole herself. The girls come in and there is a scramble at the door. Finally somebody turns the knob by mistake in the rush and the door opens, pouring Fauna and the girls into the room. Doc and Suzy break their clinch.*)

DOC: Come in!

SUZY: They are in.

FAUNA: I heard you broke your arm.

DOC: Yes, I did. But I—

MAC (*in the doorway*): Just a minute, everybody! Just a moment!

(*He whistles offstage to Jim who signals offstage to boys, who bring in a very large telescope and a very large tripod. They are followed by everyone in Cannery Row. Doc's mouth falls open. He starts to laugh and then stops.*)

Do you like it, Doc?

DOC: It's beautiful.

MAC: Biggest one in the whole damn catalogue.

DOC (*his voice choked*): Thanks, thanks, Mac. Thanks, boys. I guess after all it doesn't matter whether you look down or up as long as you look.

SUZY: Doc and me are goin' down to La Jolla tonight.

DOC: Fauna, I finally got my girl.

FAUNA: The hell you did, you were sandbagged just like everybody else.

(*Fauna starts to sing "Sweet Thursday." Everybody joins in very happily as the curtain falls.*)

SUZY

DOC